Table of Contents

Introducing Community Policing

The movement toward community policing has gained momentum in recent years as police and community leaders search for more effective ways to promote public safety and to enhance the quality of life in their neighborhoods. Chiefs, sheriffs, and other policing officials are currently assessing what changes in orientation, organization, and operations will allow them to benefit the communities they serve by improving the quality of the services they provide.

Community policing encompasses a variety of philosophical and practical approaches and is still evolving rapidly. Community policing strategies vary depending on the needs and responses of the communities involved; however, certain basic principles and considerations are common to all community policing efforts.

To date, no succinct overview of community policing exists for practitioners who want to learn to use this wide-ranging approach to address the problems of crime and disorder in their communities. Understanding Community Policing, prepared by the Community Policing Consortium, is the beginning of an effort to bring community policing into focus. The document, while not a final product, assembles and examines the critical components of community policing to help foster the learning process and to structure the experimentation and modification required to make community policing work.

Established and funded by the U.S. Department of Justice, Bureau of Justice Assistance (BJA), the Community Policing Consortium includes representatives from the International Association of Chiefs of Police (IACP), the National Sheriffs' Association, the Police Executive Research Forum (PERF), and the Police Foundation. BJA gave the Consortium the task of developing a conceptual framework for community policing and assisting agencies in implementing community policing. The process was designed to be a learning experience, allowing police, community members, and policymakers to assess the effectiveness of different implementation procedures and the impact of community policing on local levels of crime, violence, fear, and other public-safety problems.

The development of this community policing framework presented policing organizations with an opportunity to contribute to the evolution and implementation of community policing. The sharing of successes, failures, and frustrations was and will continue to be an inherent part of this process. The

Community Policing Consortium facilitates this dialog by providing direct training and technical assistance to the demonstration sites, by serving as a repository for community policing information, and by acting as a resource for State, county, and municipal police agencies interested in learning more about community policing and its implementation.

As the field of community policing evolves, BJA and the Community Policing Consortium will develop an array of products, including a community policing implementation guide, which will contain training materials with curricula, and a selection of case studies and anecdotal experiences to illustrate the challenges and results of community policing endeavors. Through BJA, the Consortium will also develop and disseminate a comprehensive resource directory and bibliography of community policing literature and practices intended to assist in future design and implementation efforts.

Understanding Community Policing provides a conceptual framework that will be useful to practitioners interested in implementing or expanding community policing initiatives. Chapter 2 describes the reasons why police professionals throughout the United States have been searching for an alternative policing strategy and traces the roots of community policing. The two defining elements of community policing—community partnership and problem solving—are examined in Chapter 3. Chapter 4 presents the basic organizational and operational elements associated with the implementation of a community policing strategy. Chapter 5 presents the criteria for assessing the progress of a community policing initiative.

As the field of community policing develops, this document will be updated and revised to reflect the transformations taking place at the test sites in this collaboration between the Bureau of Justice Assistance, the Community Policing Consortium, and the practitioner community.

Tracing the Roots of Community Policing

As defined by the Community Policing Consortium, community policing consists of two core components, community partnership and problem solving, which are both outlined in Chapter 3. The movement toward these two ideas in the United States has been initiated and shaped by concerned police executives throughout the country.

An Idea for the Times

There are compelling reasons why law enforcement leaders believe the time has come to alter the policies and practices of their organizations. These reasons are rooted in the history of policing and police research during the last quarter of a century, in the changing nature of communities, and in the shifting characteristics of crime and violence that affect these communities.

Policing strategies that worked in the past are not always effective today. The desired goal, an enhanced sense of safety, security, and well-being, has not been achieved. Practitioners agree that there is a pressing need for innovation to curb the crises in many communities. Both the level and nature of crime in this country and the changing character of American communities are causing police to seek more effective methods. Many urban communities are experiencing serious problems with illegal drugs, gang violence, murders, muggings, and burglaries. Suburban and rural communities have not escaped unscathed. They are also noting increases in crime and disorder.

In addition, the social fabric of our country has changed radically. The family unit is not as stable as it once was. Single working parents find it extremely difficult to spend enough time with their children, and churches and schools have been unable to fill this void. Immigrants, ethnic groups, and minorities, while adding to the diverse nature of American communities, often have different interests and pursue disparate goals.

Governments at all levels are having increased difficulty balancing budgets, which frequently forces police departments to allocate dwindling resources to growing problems.

In this rapidly changing environment, where police cope with an epidemic drug problem, gang activity, and increased levels of violence, the concept of community policing is taking hold. Police leaders using this commonsense

In this rapidly changing environment, . . . the concept of community policing is taking hold.

approach to the problems of crime and disorder, an approach that may very well enhance and maximize performance and resources, have struck a responsive chord in both national and local governments and in communities across the Nation.

Government and community leaders are beginning to recognize that they also must accept responsibility for keeping their neighborhoods safe. Communities must take a unified stand against crime, violence, and disregard for the law, and must make a commitment to increasing crime-prevention and intervention activities. Police agencies must help build stronger, more self-sufficient communities—communities in which crime and disorder will not thrive.

Community policing is democracy in action.

Community policing is democracy in action. It requires the active participation of local government, civic and business leaders, public and private agencies, residents, churches, schools, and hospitals. All who share a concern for the welfare of the neighborhood should bear responsibility for safeguarding that welfare. Community policing is being advocated by leaders at the highest levels of government—including President Clinton and Attorney General Reno, who describes it as the "changing of policing." In addition, it has been suggested that community policing can play a primary role in changing the way all government services are provided at the community level.

The implementation of community policing necessitates fundamental changes in the structure and management of police organizations. Community policing differs from traditional policing in how the community is perceived and in its expanded policing goals. While crime control and prevention remain central priorities, community policing strategies use a wide variety of methods to address these goals. The police and the community become partners in addressing problems of disorder and neglect (e.g., gang activity, abandoned cars, and broken windows) that, although perhaps not criminal, can eventually lead to serious crime. As links between the police and the community are strengthened over time, the ensuing partnership will be better able to pinpoint and mitigate the underlying causes of crime.

Police are finding that crime-control tactics need to be augmented with strategies that prevent crime, reduce the fear of crime, and improve the quality of life in neighborhoods. Fear of crime has become a significant problem in itself. A highly visible police presence helps reduce fear within the community, fear which has been found to be "...more closely correlated with disorder than with crime."[1] However, because fear of crime can limit activity, keep residents in their homes, and contribute to empty streets, this climate of decline can result in even greater numbers of crimes. By getting the community involved, police will have more resources available for crime-prevention activities, instead of being forced into an after-the-fact response to crime.

---

1. Kelling, George L., and Mark H. Moore. *The Evolving Strategy of Policing.* Perspectives on Policing. Washington, D.C.: National Institute of Justice and John F. Kennedy School of Government, Harvard University. 1988:p.8. Based on *The Newark Foot Patrol Experiment.* Washington, D.C.: Police Foundation. 1981.

Analyses of crime statistics show that the current emphasis on crime fighting has had a limited effect on reducing crime. In addition, the concept of centralized management of most police organizations has often served to isolate police from the communities they serve. This isolation hampers crime-fighting efforts. Statistics on unreported crime suggest that in many cases police are not aware of existing problems. Without strong ties to the community, police may not have access to pertinent information from citizens that could help solve or deter crime.

Helpful information will be forthcoming from community members when police have established a relationship of trust with the community they serve. Establishing this trust will take time, particularly in communities where internal conflicts exist or where relations with the police have been severely strained. Community policing offers a way for the police and the community to work together to resolve the serious problems that exist in these neighborhoods. Only when community members believe the police are genuinely interested in community perspectives and problems will they begin to view the police as a part of that community.

Experience and research reveal that "community institutions are the first line of defense against disorder and crime..." [2] Thus, it is essential that the police work closely with all facets of the community to identify concerns and to find the most effective solutions. This is the essence of community policing.

. . . it is essential that the police work closely with all facets of the community to identify concerns and to find the most effective solutions. This is the essence of community policing.

The Role of the Police: A Historical Perspective

When Sir Robert Peel established the London Metropolitan Police, he set forth a number of principles, one of which could be considered the seed of community policing: "...the police are the public and the public are the police." [3] For a number of reasons, the police lost sight of this relationship as the central organizing concept for police service. Researchers have suggested that the reform era in government, which began in the early 1900's, coupled with a nationwide move toward professionalization, resulted in the separation of the police from the community. [4] Police managers assigned officers to rotating shifts and moved them frequently from one geographical location to another to eliminate corruption. Management also instituted a policy of centralized control, designed to ensure compliance with standard operating procedures and to encourage a professional aura of impartiality.

---

2. As quoted in Kelling, George L. *Police and Communities: the Quiet Revolution. Perspectives on Policing.* Washington, D.C.: National Institute of Justice and John F. Kennedy School of Government, Harvard University. 1988;p.2.

3. Braiden, Chris. "Enriching Traditional Police Roles." *Police Management: Issues and Perspectives.* Washington, D.C.: Police Executive Research Forum. 1992;p.108.

4. Kelling, George L., and Mark H. Moore. *The Evolving Strategy of Policing. Perspectives on Policing.* Washington, D.C.: National Institute of Justice and John F. Kennedy School of Government, Harvard University. 1988;pp.4–5.

The police and the public had become so separated from one another that in some communities an attitude of "us versus them" prevailed between the police and community members.

This social distancing was also reinforced by technological developments. The expanding role of automobiles replaced the era of the friendly foot patrol officer. By the 1970s, rapid telephone contact with police through 911 systems allowed them to respond quickly to crimes. Answering the overwhelming number of calls for service, however, left police little time to prevent crimes from occurring. As increasingly sophisticated communications technology made it possible for calls to be transmitted almost instantaneously, officers had to respond to demands for assistance regardless of the urgency of the situation. Answering calls severely limited a broad police interaction with the community. The advent of the computer also contributed to the decrease in police contact with the community. Statistics, rather than the type of service provided or the service recipients, became the focus for officers and managers. As computers generated data on crime patterns and trends, counted the incidence of crimes, increased the efficiency of dispatch, and calculated the rapidity and outcome of police response, rapid response became an end in itself.

Random patrolling also served to further break the link between communities and police. Police were instructed to change routes constantly, in an effort to thwart criminals. However, community members also lost the ability to predict when they might be able to interact with their local police.

The height of police isolation came in an era of growing professionalization, when the prevailing ideology was that the professional knew best and when community involvement in crime control was seen by almost everyone as unnecessary.

The movement to end police corruption, the emphasis on professionalization, and the development of new technology occurred in an era of growing crime and massive social change. Police had trouble communicating with all members of the socially and culturally diverse communities they served. The police and the public had become so separated from one another that in some communities an attitude of "us versus them" prevailed between the police and community members. One observer of the urban scene characterized the deteriorating police-community relationship this way: "For the urban poor the police are those who arrest you."[5]

A Social and Professional Awakening

The burst of ideas, arguments, and protests during the 1960s and 1970s mushroomed into a full-scale social movement. Antiwar protestors, civil rights activists, and other groups began to demonstrate in order to be heard. Overburdened and poorly prepared police came to symbolize what these groups sought to change in their government and society. Focusing attention on police policies and practices became an effective way to draw attention to the

---

5. Harrington, Michael. *The Other America: Poverty in the United States.* New York: Macmillan. 1981:p.16.

need for wider change. Police became the targets of hostility, which ultimately led police leaders to concerned reflection and analysis.

In this era of protest, citizens began to take a stronger hand in the development of policies and practices that affected their lives. The police force's inability to handle urban unrest in an effective and appropriate manner brought demands by civic leaders and politicians for a reexamination of police practices. Between 1968 and 1973, three Presidential Commissions made numerous recommendations for changes in policing—recommendations that were initially responded to by outside organizations. Agencies of the U.S. Department of Justice, in collaboration with countless police departments throughout the country who were open to research and innovation, played a major role in stimulating, supporting, and disseminating research and technical assistance. Millions of dollars were spent to foster and support criminal justice education. In addition, these Federal agencies supported a wide variety of police training, conferences, research, and technology upgrading.

A number of organizations within the policing field also became committed to improving policing methods in the 1970's. Among those on the forefront of this movement for constructive change were the Police Foundation, the Police Executive Research Forum, the National Organization of Black Law Enforcement Executives, the Urban Sheriffs' Group of the National Sheriffs' Association, and the International Association of Chiefs of Police. These organizations conducted much of the basic research that led police to re-evaluate traditional policing methods.

The Role of Research in Policing

Increases in Federal funding and the growth of criminal justice education resulted in the rapid development of research on policing. Many of the research findings challenged prevailing police practices and beliefs.

Federally funded victimization surveys documented the existence of unreported crime. Practitioners had to acknowledge that only a fraction of crimes were being reported, and, therefore, began seeking ways to improve their image and to interact more effectively with the communities they served.

An early research study was the Kansas City Preventive Patrol Experiment. This field experiment found that randomized patrolling had a limited impact on crime or citizens' attitudes and caused police leaders to begin thinking about alternative ways to use their patrol personnel.[6] Another study by the Kansas City Police Department assessed the value of rapid response by police and concluded that in most cases rapid response did not help solve crimes.[7]

6. Kelling, George L., Antony Pate, Duane Dieckman, and Charles E. Brown. *The Kansas City Preventive Patrol Experiment: A Technical Report.* Washington, D.C.: Police Foundation. 1974:pp.iii, 533–5.

7. Kansas City Police Department. *Response Time Analysis: Volume II, Part I—Crime Analysis.* Washington, D.C.: U.S. Government Printing Office. 1980:p.iii.

. . . a large portion of serious crimes are not deterred by rapid response.

The study revealed that a large portion of serious crimes are not deterred by rapid response. The crime sample that was analyzed indicated that almost two-thirds of these crimes were not reported quickly enough for rapid response to be effective. While a prompt police response can increase the chance of making an onscene arrest, the time it takes a citizen to report a crime largely predetermines the effect that police response time will have on the outcome. This study revealed a need for formal call-screening procedures to differentiate between emergency and nonemergency calls. More efficient dispatching of calls could make additional time available for patrol officers to interact with the community.

This study led to further research that also demonstrated the value of response strategies that ensured that the most urgent calls received the highest priority and the most expeditious dispatch. Studies of alternative responses to calls for service found that community residents would accept responses other than the presence of police immediately on the scene if they were well informed about the types of alternatives used.[8]

Differential police response strategies were also examined by the Birmingham, Alabama, Police Department.[9] The objectives of the project were to increase the efficiency with which calls for service were managed and to improve citizen satisfaction with police service. The study included the use of call-prioritization codes, call-stacking procedures, both police and nonpolice delayed-response strategies, and teleservice. The alternate strategies were found to be successful in diverting calls from mobilized field units without a loss in citizen satisfaction.

The Directed Patrol study assessed how to use most effectively the time made available by more efficient call-response measures.[10] The study suggested that, rather than performing randomized patrols when not handling calls, the officers' time could be more profitably spent addressing specific criminal activities. To direct officers' attention and to help them secure time, the department instituted support steps that included crime analysis, teleservice, and walk-in report-handling capabilities.

The San Diego Police Department conducted several significant research studies during the 1970's. These included an evaluation of one-officer versus two-officer patrol cars, an assessment of the relationship between field interrogations of suspicious persons and criminal deterrence, and a

---

8. Eck, John E., and William Spelman. "A Problem-Oriented Approach to Police Service Delivery." *Police and Policing: Contemporary Issues,* ed. Dennis Jay Kenney. New York: Praeger. 1989:p.101.

9. Farmer, Michael T., ed. *Differential Police Response Strategies.* Washington, D.C.: Police Executive Research Forum. 1981:p.3.

10. Kansas City Police Department. *Directed Patrol: A Concept in Community-Specific, Crime-Specific, and Service-Specific Policing.* Kansas City, Missouri: Kansas City Police Department. 1974:p.465.

community-oriented policing (COP) project,[11] which was the first empirical study of community policing.

The COP project required patrol officers to become knowledgeable about their beats through "beat-profiling" activities, in which officers studied the topographics, demographics, and call histories of their beats. Officers were also expected to develop "tailored patrol" strategies to address the types of crime and citizen concerns revealed by their profiling activities.

Officers participating in the COP project concluded that random patrolling was not as important as previously thought. They also concluded that developing stronger ties with members of the community was more important than once believed. In addition, the project demonstrated that interaction with the community could improve the attitudes of officers toward their jobs and toward the communities they served and could encourage the officers to develop creative solutions to complex problems.

. . . interaction with the community can improve the attitudes of officers toward their jobs and toward the communities they serve . . . .

Many of the findings from this study have a direct bearing on contemporary community policing efforts. First, by getting to know members of the community, the officers were able to obtain valuable information about criminal activity and perpetrators. They were also able to obtain realistic assessments of the needs of community members and their expectations of police services. The study also exposed the need to reevaluate the issue of shift rotation. Officers must be assigned to permanent shifts and beats if they are to participate in community activities. Finally, the COP project demonstrated the critical role that shift lieutenants and sergeants play in program planning and implementation. The exclusion of supervisors in training and development efforts ultimately led to the demise of the COP program in San Diego.

In 1979, Herman Goldstein developed and advanced the concept of "problem-oriented policing" (POP), which encouraged police to begin thinking differently about their purpose.[12] Goldstein suggested that problem resolution constituted the true, substantive work of policing and advocated that police identify and address root causes of problems that lead to repeat calls for service. POP required a move from a reactive, incident-oriented stance to one that actively addressed the problems that continually drained police resources. In a study of POP implementation in Newport News, Virginia, POP was found to be an effective approach to addressing many community problems, and important data about POP design and implementation was gathered.[13] Other research indicated that police could identify the "hot spots"

11. Boydstun, John E., and Michael E. Sherry. San Diego Community Profile: Final Report. Washington, D.C.: Police Foundation. 1975:p.83.

12. Goldstein, Herman. "Improving Policing: A Problem-Oriented Approach." Crime and Delinquency 25(1979):pp.241–3.

13. Eck, John E., and William Spelman. Problem Solving: Problem-Oriented Policing in Newport News. Washington, D.C.: Police Executive Research Forum. 1987:pp.81,99.

of repeat calls in a community and thereby devise strategies to reduce the number of calls.[14]

While much of the policing research conducted in the 1970's dealt with patrol issues, the Rand Corporation examined the role of detectives.[15] This study concluded that detectives solved only a small percentage of the crimes analyzed and that the bulk of the cases solved hinged on information obtained by patrol officers. This dramatically challenged traditional thinking about the roles of detectives and patrol officers in the handling of investigative functions. The implication was that patrol officers should become more actively involved in criminal investigations. The implementation of appropriate training would allow patrol officers to perform some early investigating that could help in obtaining timely case closures, thereby reducing the tremendous case loads of detectives and allowing them to devote more time to complex investigations.

The Newark Foot Patrol Experiment suggested that police could develop more positive attitudes toward community members and could promote positive attitudes toward police if they spent time on foot in their neighborhoods.[16] Foot patrol also eased citizen fear of crime, "...persons living in areas where foot patrol was created perceived a notable decrease in the severity of crime-related problems."[17] Experimental foot patrols in Flint, Michigan, also elicited citizen approval. Residents said foot patrols made them feel safer and residents "...felt especially safe when the foot patrol officer was well known and highly visible."[18] In addition, it is worth noting that in both cities the use of foot patrols increased officer satisfaction with police work.[19]

The fear reduction studies provided empirical data on the effectiveness of key community policing tactics (e.g., community organizing, door-to-door

14. Sherman, Lawrence W., Patrick R. Gartin, and Michael E. Buerger. "Hot Spots of Predatory Crime: Routine Activities and the Criminology of Place." Criminology 27(1989):p.39.

15. Greenwood, Peter W., and Joan Petersilia. The Criminal Investigation Process—Volume I: Summary and Policy Implications. Santa Monica: Rand Corporation. 1975:p.v. See also Greenwood, Peter W., Jan M. Chaiken, and Joan Petersilia. The Criminal Investigation Process. Lexington: DC Heath. 1977.

16. Kelling, George L. The Newark Foot Patrol Experiment. Washington, D.C.: Police Foundation. 1981:pp.94–96.

17. Trojanowicz, Robert C. "An Evaluation of a Neighborhood Foot Patrol Program." Journal of Police Science and Administration 11(1983):pp.410–419.

18. Trojanowicz, Robert C. An Evaluation of the Neighborhood Foot Patrol Program in Flint, Michigan. East Lansing: Michigan State University. 1982:p.86. See also Trojanowicz, Robert C. "An Evaluation of a Neighborhood Foot Patrol Program." Journal of Police Science and Administration 11(1983).

19. Kelling, George L. Police and Communities: The Quiet Revolution. Perspectives on Policing. Washington, D.C.: National Institute of Justice and John F. Kennedy School of Government, Harvard University. 1988:p.5.

contacts, neighborhood mini-stations, and intensified enforcement coupled with community involvement) in reducing fear among residents, improving community conditions, and enhancing the image of the police.[20] Driving this study was the notion that if fear could be reduced, community residents would be more inclined to take an active role in preserving safety and tranquility within their neighborhoods.

Police Response to the Need for Change

A number of dynamic police leaders participated in various Presidential Commissions during the 1960's and 1970's. They also contributed their time and expertise to the newly created police organizations that were working to bring about improvements in policing policies. However, many of these police leaders found themselves alone when they tried to infuse their own departments with this spirit of change. Community policing implementation was impeded by centralized management practices and traditional operating assumptions.

Many experienced police managers and officers found it difficult to accept this challenge to the practices and procedures that had always guided their actions. Thus, it was not surprising that these innovations were often overwhelmed by traditional policies and that the innovators were frequently suspected of being manipulated by outsiders or of pursuing their personal career agendas at the expense of the organization.

Many of today's police managers have supplemented their professional education by studying literature developed since the 1970's. Once considered radical, many of the strategies that evolved from this research on policing are now considered necessary for improving performance. Ideas that were raised 20 years ago have been modified and expanded to fit current conditions.

Police executives realize that it is no longer sufficient to think in terms of making only minor alterations to traditional management and operational practices. Management's current challenge is to meet the escalating and varied demands for service with more effective delivery strategies to optimize staff and resources, to encourage innovative thinking, and to involve the community in policing efforts.

Following the lead of corporate America, police managers are beginning to adopt the principles associated with total quality or participatory management. There is growing recognition in policing that employees should have input into decisions about their work. Management practices that restrict the flow of communication and stifle innovation are giving way to the belief that those actually working in the community can best understand its needs and develop ways to meet them. Police also realize that not only the service

. . . police managers are beginning to adopt the principles associated with total quality or participatory management.

20. Pate, Antony M., Mary Ann Wycoff, Wesley G. Skogan, and Lawrence W. Sherman. *Reducing Fear of Crime in Houston and Newark: A Summary Report.* Washington, D.C.: Police Foundation. 1986:p.3.

providers but also the service recipients must define priorities and join forces with others to find inventive, long-term solutions to deepening problems of crime and violence.

Today the movement for change within policing is led aggressively by policing practitioners themselves. The current shift to community policing reflects the conscious effort of a profession to reexamine its policies and procedures. Incorporating the core components of community policing delineated in the next chapter with existing policing methods is the first step in this ongoing process.

Chapter 3

Defining the Core Components of Community Policing

The growing trend within communities to participate in the fight against crime and disorder has paralleled a growing recognition by police that traditional crime-fighting tactics alone have a limited impact on controlling crime. Community policing is the synthesis of these two movements.

The foundations of a successful community policing strategy are the close, mutually beneficial ties between police and community members. Community policing consists of two complementary core components, community partnership and problem solving. To develop community partnership, police must develop positive relationships with the community, must involve the community in the quest for better crime control and prevention, and must pool their resources with those of the community to address the most urgent concerns of community members. Problem solving is the process through which the specific concerns of communities are identified and through which the most appropriate remedies to abate these problems are found.

Community policing does not imply that police are no longer in authority or that the primary duty of preserving law and order is subordinated. However, tapping into the expertise and resources that exist within communities will relieve police of some of their burdens. Local government officials, social agencies, schools, church groups, business people—all those who work and live in the community and have a stake in its development—will share responsibility for finding workable solutions to problems that detract from the safety and security of the community.

Community policing consists of two complementary core components, community partnership and problem solving.

The Concept of Community

The goal of community policing is to reduce crime and disorder by carefully examining the characteristics of problems in neighborhoods and then applying appropriate problem-solving remedies. The "community" for which a patrol officer is given responsibility should be a small, well-defined geographical area. Beats should be configured in a manner that preserves, as much as possible, the unique geographical and social characteristics of neighborhoods while still allowing efficient service.

Effective community policing depends on optimizing positive contact between patrol officers and community members.

Patrol officers are the primary providers of police services and have the most extensive contact with community members. In community policing efforts, they will provide the bulk of the daily policing needs of the community, and they will be assisted by immediate supervisors, other police units, and appropriate government and social agencies. Upper level managers and command staff will be responsible for ensuring that the entire organization backs the efforts of patrol officers.

Effective community policing depends on optimizing positive contact between patrol officers and community members. Patrol cars are only one method of conveying police services. Police departments may supplement automobile patrols with foot, bicycle, scooter, and horseback patrols, as well as adding "mini-stations" to bring police closer to the community. Regular community meetings and forums will afford police and community members an opportunity to air concerns and find ways to address them.

Officers working long-term assignments on the same shift and beat will become familiar figures to community members and will become aware of the day-to-day workings of the community. This increased police presence is an initial move in establishing trust and serves to reduce fear of crime among community members, which, in turn, helps create neighborhood security. Fear must be reduced if community members are to participate actively in policing. People will not act if they feel that their actions will jeopardize their safety.

Although the delivery of police services is organized by geographic area, a community may encompass widely diverse cultures, values, and concerns, particularly in urban settings. A community consists of more than just the local government and the neighborhood residents. Churches, schools, hospitals, social groups, private and public agencies, and those who work in the area are also vital members of the community. In addition, those who visit for cultural or recreational purposes or provide services to the area are also concerned with the safety and security of the neighborhood. Including these "communities of interest" in efforts to address problems of crime and disorder can expand the resource base of the community.

Concerns and priorities will vary within and among these communities of interest. Some communities of interest are long-lasting and were formed around racial, ethnic, occupational lines, or a common history, church, or school. Others form and reform as new problems are identified and addressed. Interest groups within communities can be in opposition to one another—sometimes in violent opposition. Intracommunity disputes have been common in large urban centers, especially in times of changing demographics and population migrations.

These multiple and sometimes conflicting interests require patrol officers to function not only as preservers of law and order, but also as skillful mediators. Demands on police from one community of interest can sometimes clash with the rights of another community of interest. For example, a community group may oppose certain police tactics used to crack down on gang activity, which the group believes may result in discriminatory arrest practices. The police must not only protect the rights of the protesting group, but must also work with all of the community members involved to find a way to preserve neighborhood peace. For this process to be effective, community members must communicate their views and suggestions and back up the negotiating efforts of the police. In this way, the entire community participates in the mediation process and helps preserve order. The police must encourage a spirit of cooperation that balances the collective interests of all citizens with the personal rights of individuals.

The conflicts within communities are as important as the commonalities. Police must recognize the existence of both to build the cooperative bonds needed to maintain order, provide a sense of security, and control crime. Police must build lasting relationships that encompass all elements of the community and center around the fundamental issues of public safety and quality of life. The key to managing this difficult task is trust.

Establishing and maintaining mutual trust is the central goal of community partnership.

Community Partnership: Core Component One

Establishing and maintaining mutual trust is the central goal of the first core component of community policing—community partnership. Police recognize the need for cooperation with the community. In the fight against serious crime, police have encouraged community members to come forth with relevant information. In addition, police have spoken to neighborhood groups, participated in business and civic events, worked with social agencies, and taken part in educational and recreational programs for school children. Special units have provided a variety of crisis intervention services. So how then do the cooperative efforts of community policing differ from the actions that have taken place previously? The fundamental distinction is that, in community policing, the police become an integral part of the community culture, and the community assists in defining future priorities and in allocating resources. The difference is substantial and encompasses basic goals and commitments.

Community partnership means adopting a policing perspective that exceeds the standard law enforcement emphasis. This broadened outlook recognizes the value of activities that contribute to the orderliness and well-being of a neighborhood. These activities could include: helping accident or crime victims, providing emergency medical services, helping resolve domestic and neighborhood conflicts (e.g., family violence, landlord-tenant disputes, or racial harassment), working with residents and local businesses to improve neighborhood conditions, controlling automobile and pedestrian traffic, providing emergency social services and referrals to those at risk (e.g., adolescent runaways, the homeless, the intoxicated, and the mentally ill), protecting the exercise of constitutional rights (e.g., guaranteeing a person's right to speak, protecting lawful assemblies from disruption), and providing a model of citizenship (helpfulness, respect for others, honesty, and fairness).

These services help develop trust between the police and the community. This trust will enable the police to gain greater access to valuable information from the community that could lead to the solution and prevention of crimes, will engender support for needed crime-control measures, and will provide an opportunity for officers to establish a working relationship with the community. The entire police organization must be involved in enlisting the cooperation of community members in promoting safety and security.

Building trust will not happen overnight; it will require ongoing effort. But trust must be achieved before police can assess the needs of the community and construct the close ties that will engender community support. In turn, as Figure 1 illustrates, this cooperative relationship will deepen the bonds of trust.

To build this trust for an effective community partnership police must treat people with respect and sensitivity. The use of unnecessary force and arrogance, aloofness, or rudeness at any level of the agency will dampen the willingness of community members to ally themselves with the police.

The effective mobilization of community support requires different approaches in different communities. Establishing trust and obtaining cooperation are often easier in middle-class and affluent communities than in poorer communities, where mistrust of police may have a long history. Building bonds in some neighborhoods may involve supporting basic social institutions (e.g., families, churches, schools) that have been weakened by pervasive crime or disorder.[21] The creation of viable communities is necessary if lasting alliances that nurture cooperative efforts are to be sustained. Under community policing, the police become both catalysts and facilitators in the development of these communities.

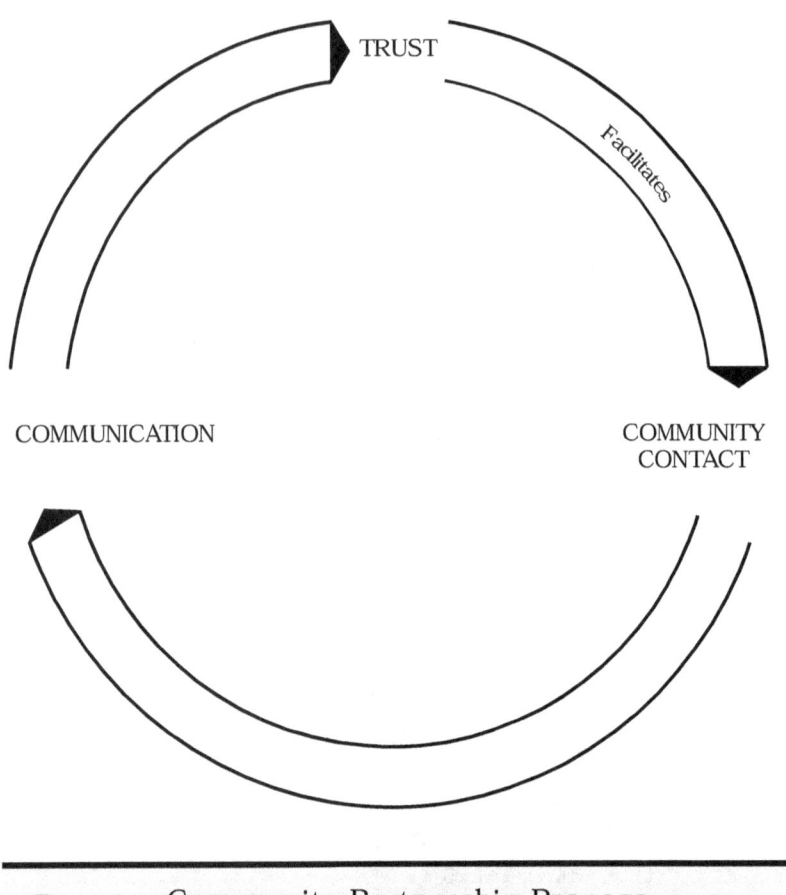

Figure 1   Community Partnership Process

21. Moore, Mark H., Robert Trojanowicz, and George L. Kelling. Crime and Policing, Perspectives on Policing. Washington, D.C.: National Institute of Justice and John F. Kennedy School of Government, Harvard University. 1988:p.10.

Community policing expands police efforts to prevent and control crime. The community is no longer viewed by police as a passive presence or a source of limited information, but as a partner in this effort. Community concerns with crime and disorder thus become the target of efforts by the police and the community working in tandem.

The close alliance forged with the community should not be limited to an isolated incident or series of incidents, nor confined to a specific time frame. The partnership between the police and the community must be enduring and balanced. It must break down the old concepts of professional versus civilian, expert versus novice, and authority figure versus subordinate. The police and the community must be collaborators in the quest to encourage and preserve peace and prosperity.

The police and the community must be collaborators in the quest to encourage and preserve peace and prosperity.

The more conspicuous police presence of the long-term patrol officer in itself may encourage community response. But it is not sufficient. The entire police organization must vigorously enlist the cooperation of community residents in pursuing the goals of deterring crime and preserving order. Police personnel on every level must join in building a broad rapport with community members.

For the patrol officer, police/community partnership entails talking to local business owners to help identify their problems and concerns, visiting residents in their homes to offer advice on security, and helping to organize and support neighborhood watch groups and regular community meetings. For example, the patrol officer will canvass the neighborhood for information about a string of burglaries and then revisit those residents to inform them when the burglar is caught. The chief police executive will explain and discuss controversial police tactics so that community members understand the necessity of these tactics for public and officer safety. The department management will consult community members about gang suppression tactics, and every level of the department will actively solicit the concerns and suggestions of community groups, residents, leaders, and local government officials. In this police/community partnership, providing critical social services will be acknowledged as being inextricably linked to deterring crime, and problem solving will become a cooperative effort.

Problem Solving: Core Component Two

Problem solving is a broad term that implies more than simply the elimination and prevention of crimes. Problem solving is based on the assumption that "crime and disorder can be reduced in small geographic areas by carefully studying the characteristics of problems in the area, and then applying the appropriate resources..." and on the assumption that "Individuals make choices based on the opportunities presented by the immediate physical and social characteristics of an area. By manipulating these factors, people will be less inclined to act in an offensive manner."[22]

The problem-solving process is explained further:

> The theory behind problem-oriented policing is simple. Underlying conditions create problems. These conditions might include the characteristics of the people involved (offenders, potential victims, and others), the social setting in which these people interact, the physical environments, and the way the public deals with these conditions.
>
> A problem created by these conditions may generate one or more incidents. These incidents, while stemming from a common source, may appear to be different. For example, social and physical conditions in a deteriorated apartment complex may generate burglaries, acts of vandalism, intimidation of pedestrians by rowdy teenagers, and other incidents. These incidents, some of which come to police attention, are symptoms of the problems. The incidents will continue so long as the problem that creates them persists.[23]

Determining the underlying causes of crime depends, to a great extent, on an indepth knowledge of community.

As police recognize the effectiveness of the problem-solving approach, there is a growing awareness that community involvement is essential for its success. Determining the underlying causes of crime depends, to a great extent, on an indepth knowledge of community. Therefore, community participation in identifying and setting priorities will contribute to effective problem-solving efforts by the community and the police. Cooperative problem solving also reinforces trust, facilitates the exchange of information, and leads to the identification of other areas that could benefit from the mutual attention of the police and the community. As Figure 2 illustrates, the problem-solving process, like community partnership, is self-renewing.

For this process to operate effectively the police need to devote attention to and recognize the validity of community concerns. Neighborhood groups and the police will not always agree on which specific problems deserve attention first. Police may regard robberies as the biggest problem in a particular community, while residents may find derelicts who sleep in doorways, break bottles on sidewalks, and pick through garbage cans to be the number one problem. Under community policing, the problem with derelicts should also receive early attention from the police with the assistance of other government agencies and community members. For example, one police captain reported the following:

---

22. Eck, John E., and William Spelman, et al. *Problem Solving: Problem-Oriented Policing in Newport News.* Washington, D.C.: Police Executive Research Forum. 1987:pp.xvi–xvii. See also Clarke, Ronald V. "Situational Crime Prevention: Its Theoretical Basis and Practical Scope." *Crime and Justice: An Annual Review of Research,* eds. Michael Tonry and Norval Morris. Chicago: University of Chicago Press. 1983.

23. Eck, John E., and William Spelman, et al. *Problem Solving: Problem-Oriented Policing in Newport News.* Washington, D.C.: Police Executive Research Forum. 1987:p.xvi.

What we found . . . was that maybe some things that we thought were important to them really weren't that important, and other things we didn't think were important at all, were very important . . . Like abandoned cars: in one of our areas, that was a very important thing. They were really bugged about all these abandoned cars, and they thought it was a bad police department that wouldn't take care of them. When we started removing the cars their opinion of us went up, even though because we'd changed priorities we were putting fewer drug addicts in jail.[24]

Therefore, in addition to the serious crime problems identified by police, community policing must also address the problems of significant concern to the community. Community policing in effect allows community members to bring problems of great concern to them to the attention of the police. Once informed of community concerns, the police must work with citizens to address them, while at the same time encouraging citizens to assist in solving the problems of concern to the police.

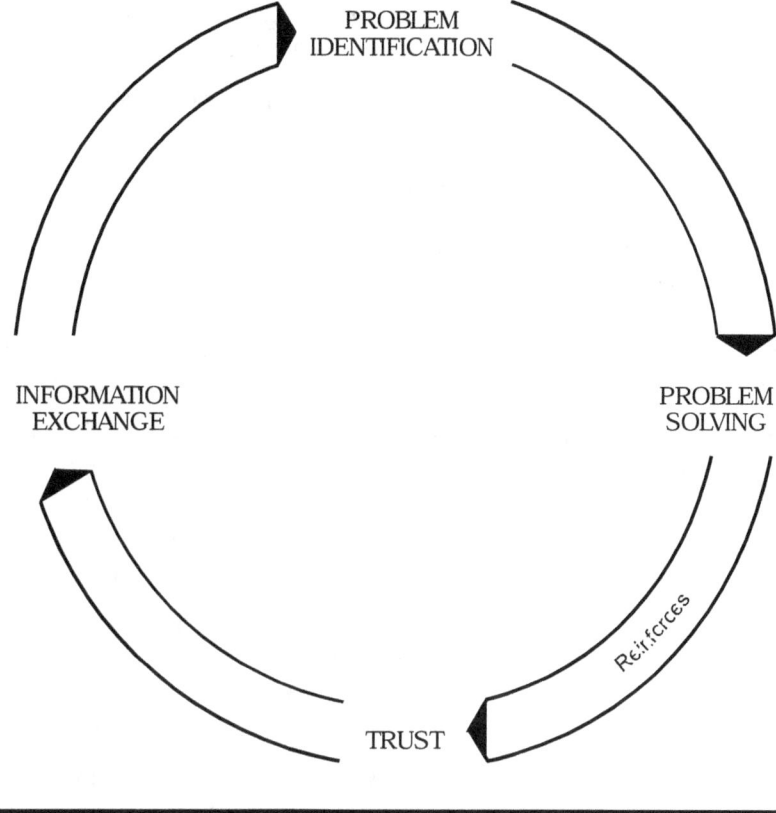

Figure 2   Problem-Solving Process

The nature of community problems will vary widely and will often involve multiple incidents that are related by factors including geography, time, victim or perpetrator group, and environment. Problems can affect a small area of a community, an entire community, or many communities. Community problems might include the following:

n An unusually high number of burglaries in an apartment complex that are creating great anxiety and fear among residents.

n Panhandling that creates fear in a business district.

n Prostitutes in local parks or on heavily traveled streets.

24. Sparrow, Malcolm K., Mark H. Moore, and David M. Kennedy. Beyond 911: A New Era in Policing. New York: Basic Books. 1990:pp.175–176.

n   Disorderly youth who regularly assemble in the parking lot of a convenience store.

n   An individual who persistently harasses and provokes community members.[25]

In community policing, the problem-solving process is dependent on input from both the police and the community. Problem solving can involve:

Problem solving is limited only by the imagination, creativity, perseverance, and enthusiasm of those involved.

n   Eliminating the problem entirely. This type of solution is usually limited to disorder problems. Examples include eliminating traffic congestion by erecting traffic control signs, and destroying or rehabilitating abandoned buildings that can provide an atmosphere conducive to crime.

n   Reducing the number of the occurrences of the problem. Drug-dealing and the accompanying problems of robbery and gang violence will be decreased if the police and community work together to set up drug counseling and rehabilitation centers. Longer range solutions might include intensifying drug education in schools, churches, and hospitals.

n   Reducing the degree of injury per incident. For example, police can teach store clerks how to act during a robbery in order to avoid injury or death and can advise women in the community on ways to minimize the chances of being killed or seriously injured if attacked.

n   Improving problem handling. Police should always make an effort to treat people humanely, (e.g., show sensitivity in dealing with rape victims and seek ways to ease their trauma, or increase effectiveness in handling runaway juveniles, drug addicts, drunk drivers, etc., by working with other agencies more closely).

n   Manipulating environmental factors to discourage criminal behavior. This can include collaborative efforts to add better lighting, remove overgrown weeds and trim shrubbery, and seal off vacant apartment buildings.

There are as many solutions as there are problems. These solutions range from simple, inexpensive measures to complex, long-term answers that will require significant investment of staff and resources. Problem solving is limited only by the imagination, creativity, perseverance, and enthusiasm of those involved. Community policing allows solutions to be tailor-made to the specific concerns of each community. The best solutions are those that satisfy community members, improve safety, diminish anxiety, lead to increased order, strengthen the ties between the community and the police, and minimize coercive actions. The following example describes such a solution:

A patrol officer faced with chronic nighttime robberies of convenience stores discovered that a major contributing factor was that cash registers could not be seen from the street, either because of their location within the store or because of posters plastered on front windows. The officer

---

25. Goldstein, Herman. *Problem-Oriented Policing.* New York: McGraw Hill. 1990.pp.66–67.

did not identify the "root cause" or ultimate cause of crime, but instead identified an underlying condition that, once addressed, held promise of reducing the number of future convenience store robberies.

To identify this underlying problem, the patrol officer talked with and solicited suggestions from convenience store owners and employees, other members of the business community, and community residents. The officer's identification of a contributing cause of the robberies is a high-leverage accomplishment in terms of its likely positive impact on the frequency of future robberies. Evidence of police concern and soliciting input from the community also reinforces cooperative ties.[26]

Patrol officers serve as catalysts for joint police and community problem-solving endeavors.

Patrol officers serve as catalysts for joint police and community problem-solving endeavors. They are involved with the community on a day-to-day basis, understand its unique physical and social characteristics, are aware of local problems, and when needed can help community members articulate their needs. Many problems within the community can be successfully handled by patrol officers or their immediate supervisors and members of the community—e.g., determining that better lighting would decrease the incidence of muggings at a local park.

All levels of the police organization should contribute to problem solving, depending on the scope and seriousness of the problem. For example, crafting a solution to widespread incidents of spousal assault taking place in several communities in an agency's jurisdiction might involve multiple levels of police management. Patrol officers may have noticed a correlation between spousal assaults and excessive drinking by the perpetrators, especially at illegal after-hours clubs. The officers, their supervisors, and community members might explore ways to close down these clubs with the help of local zoning and city planning boards. Perpetrators with alcohol problems might be required to attend rehabilitation programs run by a city agency. Meanwhile, mid- and senior-level police managers and community leaders might confer with women's groups and other social agencies about providing temporary housing and counseling for victims and their families. In addition, members of the community might be able to repair an abandoned building to house the victims.

The problem-solving process relies on the expertise and assistance of an array of social and government agencies and community resources. At the senior command level, police managers might combine forces with a civil abatement agency to condemn and board up crack houses. One police officer seeking a systemwide approach to the problem of spousal assault formed a team comprised of units from the police department and representatives from women's shelters, the YWCA, nearby military bases, the prosecutor's office, newspapers, hospitals, and social agencies. A tremendous amount of leverage

---

26. Dietz and Baker. "Murder at Work." *American Journal of Public Health* 77(1987): pp.273-274.

can be attained through the collaboration and partnership of this type of far-ranging alliance.

Community policing puts new emphasis on tackling the underlying causes of crime by addressing problems at the grassroots level. To maximize the time that the patrol officer can spend interacting with community members, community policing encourages the use of the 911 system only for true emergencies. Nonemergency calls should be handled through other means, including delays in responding and report handling by the police station or sheriff's office over the telephone or by mail.

Community policing emphasizes the value of the patrol function and the patrol officer as an individual.

These alternative measures require a wide base of support within the community. To obtain this support, the police must instruct residents on the nature of an emergency and on alternative responses to nonemergencies. Alternative responses will need to be thoroughly explained before community members will accept them. The residents should be secure in the knowledge that the police response will be appropriate for the urgency of the demand for service, and that the reduction in the volume of 911 calls will allow officers to spend more time in the community and will maximize the use of the residents' tax dollars.

Implications for Management and the Organizational Structure

Effective community partnership and problem solving will require the mastery of new responsibilities and the adoption of a flexible style of management. Community policing emphasizes the value of the patrol function and the patrol officer as an individual. Patrol officers have traditionally been accorded low status despite the scope and sensitivity of the tasks they perform. Community policing requires the shifting of initiative, decisionmaking, and responsibility downward within the police organization. The neighborhood officer or deputy sheriff becomes responsible for managing the delivery of services to a community, and ". . . everything of a policing nature [in that community] 'belongs' to that person."[27]

With this responsibility comes wide-ranging discretionary and decisionmaking power. Under community policing, patrol officers are given broader freedom to decide what should be done and how it should be done in their communities—they assume managerial responsibility for the delivery of police services to their assigned area. Patrol officers are the most familiar with the needs and strengths of their communities and are thus in the best position to forge the close ties with the community that lead to effective solutions to local problems.

The shift in status and duties of the patrol officer is critical to the community partnership and problem-solving components of community policing.

---

27. Braiden, Chris R. "Enriching Traditional Roles." *Police Management: Issues and Perspectives,* ed. Larry T. Hoover. Washington, D.C.: Police Executive Research Forum. 1992:p.101.

Assignment stability of these neighborhood officers is also essential if they are to develop close working relationships within their communities because

> . . . they are expected to engage in activities other than simply reacting to calls for service. Having officers periodically rotate among the shifts impedes their ability to identify problems. It also discourages creative solutions to impact the problems, because the officers end up rotating away from the problems. Thus, a sense of responsibility to identify and resolve problems is lost. Likewise, management cannot hold the officers accountable to deal with problems if the officers are frequently rotated from one shift to another.[28]

The enhanced role of the patrol officer has enormous organizational and managerial implications. The entire police organization must be structured, managed, and operated in a manner that supports the efforts of the patrol officer and that encourages a cooperative approach to solving problems. Under community policing, command is no longer centralized, and many decisions now come from the bottom up instead of from the top down. Greater decisionmaking power is given to those closest to the situation with the expectation that this change will improve the overall performance of the agency. This transformation in command structure is not only sound management, but is also crucial to the creation of meaningful and productive ties between the police and the community. To establish a partnership with the community,

> . . . the police must move to empower two groups: the public itself and the street officers who serve it most closely and regularly. Only when the public has a real voice in setting police priorities will its needs be taken seriously; only when street officers have the operational latitude to take on the problems they encounter with active departmental backing will those needs really be addressed.[29]

Community policing alters the contemporary functions of supervisors and managers. Under community policing, management serves to guide, rather than dominate, the actions of patrol officers and to ensure that officers have the necessary resources to solve the problems in their communities. Creativity and innovation must be fostered if satisfactory solutions to long-standing community problems are to be found.

The transition to community policing requires recognizing that the new responsibilities and decisionmaking power of the neighborhood patrol officers must be supported, guided, and encouraged by the entire organization. In addition, it requires establishing clearly stated values that provide both the

Creativity and innovation must be fostered if satisfactory solutions to long-standing community problems are to be found.

28. Oettmeier, Timothy N., and William H. Bieck. *Developing a Policing Style for Neighborhood Policing.* Executive Session #1. Houston: Houston Police Department. 1987:pp.12–13.

29. Sparrow, Malcolm K., Mark H. Moore, and David M. Kennedy. *Beyond 911: A New Era for Policing.* New York: Basic Books. 1990:pp.182–183.

police organization and the public with a clear sense of policing's expanded focus and direction.

Values: The Guiding Principles

Community policing is ultimately about values—specifically, the change in values that is needed to adapt policing to these changing times. Values must be ingrained in the very culture of the organization and must be reflected in its objectives, in its policies, and in the actions of its personnel.

> Values are the beliefs that guide an organization and the behavior of its employees ....The most important beliefs are those that set forth the ultimate purposes of the organization ....They provide the organization with its raison d'etre for outsiders and insiders alike and justify the continuing investment in the organization's enterprise . . . . [They] influence substantive and administrative decisions facing the organization, they lend a coherence and predictability to top management's actions and the responses to the actions of employees. This helps employees make proper decisions and use their discretion with confidence that they are contributing to rather than detracting from organizational performance.[30]

A clear statement of beliefs and goals gives direction to the organization and helps ensure that values are transformed into appropriate actions and behaviors.

A clear statement of beliefs and goals gives direction to the organization and helps ensure that values are transformed into appropriate actions and behaviors. The entire agency must be committed to the values embodied by such a mission statement. This mission statement should be widely disseminated both inside and outside the police organization to garner public support and to facilitate accountability. In the move to community policing, where problem-solving efforts and accountability are shared by the police, the local government, and the community, explicitly defined values become critically important in assigning responsibility and attracting and mobilizing support and resources. Community policing

> . . . relies heavily on the articulation of policing values that incorporate citizen involvement in matters that directly affect the safety and quality of neighborhood life. The culture of the police department therefore becomes one that not only recognizes the merits of community involvement but also seeks to organize and manage departmental affairs in ways that are consistent with such beliefs.[31]

30. Wasserman, Robert, and Mark H. Moore. Values in Policing. Perspectives on Policing. Washington, D.C.: National Institute of Justice and John F. Kennedy School of Government, Harvard University. 1988:pp.1,3.

31. Brown, Lee P. Community Policing: A Practical Guide for Police Officials. Perspectives on Policing. Washington, D.C.: National Institute of Justice and John F. Kennedy School of Government, Harvard University. 1989:p.5.

An organization's mission statement should be simple, direct, and unassuming. Values must be unequivocally communicated so that officers understand the influence on their actions:

> Planners need to assess what specific behaviors by organizational members support or undermine the stated values. This assessment requires that the values be defined in operational terms such that an observer can know whether any particular employee action is on target or off target . . . . Planners must also think clearly about how management will know whether the desired changes are taking place; feedback and evaluative steps must be developed.[32]

Community policing relies on the establishment of a clear, unambiguous link of values to behaviors. By creating a system of performance measurement, specific operational meaning can be given to seemingly abstract values. The guiding values central to community policing are trust, cooperation, communication, ingenuity, integrity, initiative, discretion, leadership, responsibility, respect, and a broadened commitment to public safety and security. A succinct mission statement that embodies these values and that is widely communicated to personnel, local government, and members of the community will form the basis of assessment systems that match actions and behaviors to the goals of community policing.

---

32. Cordner, Gary W., Craig B. Fraser, and Chuck Wexler. "Research, Planning, and Implementation." Local Government Police Management, ed. William A. Geller. Washington, D.C.: International City Management Association. 3d edition. 1991:pp.346–347.

Implementing a Community Policing Strategy

The implementation of a community policing strategy is a complicated and multifaceted process that, in essence, requires planning and managing for change. Community policing cannot be established through a mere modification of existing policy; profound changes must occur on every level and in every area of a police agency—from patrol officer to chief executive and from training to technology. A commitment to community policing must guide every decision and every action of the department.

Some Implementation Basics

Implementation plans will vary from agency to agency and from community to community. The most appropriate implementation method will depend, in part, on internal and external conditions facing the agency. For example, a chief executive who comes into an organization that is ripe for change at a time when confidence in the police is low may find that the organization will respond favorably to innovative policies. On the other hand, a chief executive who inherits a smoothly running organization may find it more difficult to implement change.[33]

One factor that will affect the approach to implementation is the extent of change that is required. In some agencies, current operations procedures and management practices may already conform closely to community policing, while in others extensive changes may be necessary. This will affect how a chief guides the organization toward the goals of community policing. A thorough assessment of current programs will help identify what will be required to integrate community partnership and problem-solving strategies and expanded crime control and prevention tactics with preexisting policies. Identifying priorities for change will also permit police agencies to establish interim milestones for monitoring progress.

Another essential element of successful implementation is communication. Communication must be timely, comprehensive, and direct. The chief

33. Sparrow, Malcolm K. *Implementing Community Policing.* Perspectives on Policing. Washington, D.C.: National Institute of Justice and John F. Kennedy School of Government, Harvard University. 1988: p.2.

Ongoing input, evaluation, and feedback from both inside and outside the police organization are essential to making community policing work.

executive must explain the concepts of community policing thoroughly to the entire police organization, the local political leadership, public and private agencies, and the community at large. All participants must understand their role in community policing efforts. Regular communication will encourage active participation and decrease resistance and opposition. Lines of communication must be maintained both within the police organization and between the police and participants within the community. Successful implementation requires the smooth flow of information.

The implementation of a community policing strategy must be a dynamic and flexible process. Ongoing input, evaluation, and feedback from both inside and outside the police organization are essential to making community policing work. All phases of community policing implementation must be carefully planned and properly timed to maximize success; even good ideas can fail if they are poorly executed.

Planning must be responsive to changing needs, conditions, and priorities. A strong research and planning capability that is open to suggestion and criticism will allow refinements and revisions to be made during the implementation process. Such flexibility is crucial to the success of community policing.

There are numerous ways in which police management can steer agencies toward community policing. This chapter offers guidelines that can be adapted to the circumstances of different organizations and communities.

City and Community Resources

The long-term success of community policing in transforming the law enforcement profession depends on the willingness of local governments to pursue effective integration. Elected and appointed administrators must understand the law enforcement agency's implementation strategy and participate in its development. Mayors, city managers, legislative representatives, and other government executives must not be passive partners in this process; they must guide the expansion of this movement toward "community-oriented government" at the local level. Just as the police need to determine the best ways to respond to and solve problems of crime and violence, political leaders and service providers need to find ways to direct all available resources at these critical social problems. Law enforcement agencies alone do not have the resources to address all contemporary problems; however, community policing can be a catalyst for mobilizing resources at the national, State, and local levels to impact these problems more successfully.

Collaboration between the police agency and local government officials is essential, since officers and supervisors will routinely seek assistance from local government departments for services from sanitation to health. Regular communication with the heads of government agencies will help secure their assistance and will allow them to prepare their personnel for the additional service requests that will be received.

Nongovernment agencies and institutions constitute another important community asset. The chief or sheriff should enlist the support of these private agencies in community policing efforts. One department invited representatives from these organizations to participate in training sessions on community-oriented policing.[34]

Depending on the nature and scope of the problem addressed, the composition of problem-solving teams could be restricted to police personnel or could include representatives from the community, government agencies, and social agencies. The department must develop close cooperative links with all community policing partners who contribute to the problem-solving process, and explicit procedures must be established that facilitate the appropriate use of resources.

Every member of the police organization can contribute to the development of a comprehensive list of available government and private resources. This list should include names, addresses, phone numbers, and a description of services. This information should be easily accessible to allow patrol officers, supervisors, and dispatchers to provide references to community members.

Plan of Action: Three Options

There is no "right" way to implement community policing. Each of the following three approaches has strengths and weaknesses.

Plan, then implement. This method entails developing a detailed long-range plan, with tasks and timelines, and assigning officers to execute the plan. This approach clearly delineates a set of strategies and actions that impart a sense of direction to implementation efforts; however, the initial planning stage for a large agency can take months or even years, and even a very detailed plan will be unable to predict the obstacles that will arise. In the absence of experience-based feedback, some part of the implementation process may be miscalculated.

Planning can also be complicated by the size of the staff involved. Keeping the planning staff relatively small may prevent the process from becoming unwieldy; however, it may not adequately represent all levels of command, function, and experience within the organization, thus creating the risk that the plan will not be well implemented. Planning can also become excessive and may stifle enthusiasm.

Plan and implement. In this approach, planning and action occur simultaneously. While the planning process continues, the agency begins to implement certain aspects of the program. This method allows the agency to get started quickly, involves more personnel at the outset, and permits future planning to benefit from feedback. However, the agency risks false starts,

---

34. Couper, David C., and Sabine H. Lobitz. Quality Policing: The Madison Experience. Washington, D.C.: Police Executive Research Forum. 1991:p.67.

confusion, and major blunders unless effective, rapid, and regular communication takes place between planners and implementers.

Implement with little planning. The third option is for an agency with little preparation or knowledge of the nature of community policing to quickly launch into the action phase and then, on the basis of feedback, to retool the effort and begin the cycle again. This process is continuous, with each reevaluation cycle advancing the idea of community policing a bit further within the organization. This approach assumes that a limited knowledge of community policing may prevent agencies from initially planning in a meaningful way. Advocates note that the almost immediate action will catch officers' attention at all organizational levels and will harness the existing enthusiasm to help mobilize support. However, the constant shifts in goals and actions can be highly unsettling to the organization and the community it serves.

Among the factors to be considered when selecting a method of implementation are the extent of change in current agency operations that will be required, the size of the organization, the staff the agency can assign to implementation efforts, the readiness of the organization for the new approach, and the expectations of the community. The method of planning and implementing simultaneously will probably prove most effective for the majority of agencies implementing community policing.

Scope of Initial Implementation Efforts

Initial implementation of community policing can involve the entire agency, or only a special unit or district. Agencywide commitment will require a reevaluation of all aspects of operations. Many systems will need to be restructured to facilitate new job responsibilities and to foster productive partnerships with the community. Initiating changes of this magnitude will require patience, perseverance, and total commitment. For these reasons, organizationwide implementation may not be feasible for agencies in which current methods of policing are deeply ingrained. Effective implementation will require time to train personnel, establish bonds with the community, and create appropriate support systems. The amount of time required will depend on the current orientation of the organization, its existing relationship with the community, and the resources available.

Implementation of community policing through a special, well-trained unit often offers early indications of success and focuses the attention of the community and media on the beneficial nature of community policing. However, care must be taken to avoid creating divisions within the agency. If community policing is perceived as merely a special-unit function, its eventual implementation throughout the agency could be significantly impaired. In addition, launching community policing through a special unit can lead to the misconception that the new policing style does not have to be integrated with all other facets of operations.

Implementation within one or more districts or areas can serve to demonstrate success and generate valuable data for expanding community policing agencywide, but this may also require more time and effort than implementation within a special unit. However, officers in the targeted district can help train others as community policing expands throughout the organization. Another advantage of district implementation is that it requires the cooperative efforts of all levels of management. The community policing district must not be perceived as a mere adjunct to existing police procedures.

The effectiveness of the implementation of community policing throughout the organization will depend on the manner in which community policing goals are communicated initially. If agency leaders imply that community policing in the special unit or district constitutes a test to determine whether the approach should be expanded agencywide, competition and divisiveness can result. Managers should state unequivocally that the special unit or district is not a test site, but is the starting point for the agencywide implementation of community policing.

No matter which approach is selected, feedback is essential. Without adequate feedback, agencies can encounter implementation problems that could have been avoided. Mistakes are bound to occur during implementation of community policing. Recognizing mistakes, handling them in a timely manner, and learning from them should be built into well-planned feedback procedures.

Change must come from the top down. The behavior of the chief executive will set the tone and pattern for the entire organization.

Mobilizing Support

The police executive will be called on to display exemplary leadership in the move to community policing. Change must come from the top down. The behavior of the chief executive will set the tone and pattern for the entire organization. Management must create a new, unified organizational outlook, and strategies must be developed to deal effectively with obstacles to change.

> For the police it is an entirely different way of life ....The task facing the police chief is nothing less than to change the fundamental culture of the organization ....Throughout the period of change the office of the chief executive is going to be surrounded by turbulence, like it or not. It will require personal leadership of considerable strength and perseverance.[35]

Early mobilization of support for community policing is critical. Internally, the chief or sheriff must develop support at all levels of the organization; externally, the chief executives must gather support from the local government, public and private agencies, the media, and other policing agencies in the region. The cooperation of the local mayor or city manager is imperative to

---

35. Sparrow, Malcolm K. *Implementing Community Policing.* Perspectives on Policing. Washington, D.C.: National Institute of Justice and John F. Kennedy School of Government, Harvard University. 1988:p.2.

A certain amount of opposition to community policing should be anticipated, both inside and outside the agency.

the successful implementation of a community policing strategy, as is the cooperation of local government decisionmakers and community organizations. A lack of commitment from any of these key groups could result in failure.

A certain amount of opposition to community policing should be anticipated, both inside and outside the agency. Elected officials may be too impatient to await the results of a community policing effort or may prefer to have a newer version of current policing procedures. Some groups within the community may be suspicious of the concept in general.

Resistance within the agency is inevitable as restructuring occurs. During the implementation of any change, employees may feel threatened and seek ways to resist.[36] This will be especially true if community policing is incorrectly perceived as being "soft on crime" and as making social service activities the patrol officers' primary responsibility.

Those at the highest level of command must be aware of the concerns of mid-level managers, who may be particularly sensitive to the shifts in decisionmaking responsibility and to the wider discretion accorded patrol officers.

> Teamwork, flexibility, mutual participation in decisionmaking, and citizen satisfaction are concepts that initially may threaten the supervisor who is more comfortable with the authoritarian role and routinized operations inherent in traditional policing. Thus, the education of supervisors in new styles of leadership and management must be given a high priority if they are to carry out their responsibility for the success of community policing.[37]

Keeping all personnel well informed, involving them in ongoing planning and implementation, soliciting their input and suggestions, and encouraging feedback in all areas of implementation are essential to obtaining organizationwide support. Management must instill the agency with a new spirit of trust and cooperation that will be carried over into the relationships between the agency and its community policing partners. The early cooperation and influence of management is key to gaining support throughout the ranks.

> Chiefs who do not invest in assessing and responding to the honest attitudes of managers, who do not invest in defining the new roles managers are expected to play, and who do not provide their managers with the training they need to effectively fill these new roles are likely to

---

36. Cordner, Gary W., Craig B. Fraser, and Chuck Wexler. "Research, Planning and Implementation." Local Government Police Management, ed. William A. Geller. Washington, D.C.: International City Management Association. 3d edition. 1991.

37. Meese, Edwin III. Community Policing and the Police Officer. Perspectives on Policing. Washington, D.C.: National Institute of Justice and John F. Kennedy School of Government, Harvard University. 1991:p.7.

be frustrated in their efforts to implement change. In their frustration with managers, they will be tempted to bypass them and to go straight to the first-line officers with implementation plans....But without the support of the supervisors and managers, few first-line officers will be willing to risk changing their behaviors.[38]

Agency leaders can also move to counter intraagency resistance by building a strong external constituency.[39] The chief or sheriff might make a public commitment to community policing and elicit from special interest groups a statement of their concerns. The chief may be able to support the work of commissions and committees that support ideas for change. These efforts would allow the top management to approach the organization backed by a public mandate for community policing.

In anticipation of a move to community policing, a chief might also disband some squads that emphasize traditional methods of policing, redesign evaluation systems to give credit for contributions to the nature and quality of community life, expand training to include community partnership and problem-solving strategies, and establish new communication channels with other public service organizations.[40]

Timing

Timing is an important factor in the implementation process. Implementation that moves too slowly may dampen enthusiasm and reduce momentum, while implementation that moves too quickly may create confusion and resentment and may threaten the success of the project through the use of hurried and ill-conceived methods. Community policing requires major changes in operations including: decentralization of activities and facilities, role changes for most personnel, new training, revised schedules, and an altered call-response system. All of these changes require careful consideration and coordination.

> The order of some changes will have an inherent logic; it simply won't make sense to undertake some before making others. However, the ordering of some of the objectives may be optional. When this is the case, it may make sense to postpone the more difficult until later in the change timetable. Easy "wins" may make the best openers. These would be changes for which it should be possible to build the broadest base of

38. Wycoff, Mary Ann and Timothy Oettmeier. Forthcoming. 1994.

39. Sparrow, Malcolm K. Implementing Community Policing. Perspectives on Policing. Washington, D.C.: National Institute of Justice and John F. Kennedy School of Government, Harvard University. 1988:p.3.

40. Ibid.

support... . Meeting some of the easier goals may help prepare the organization for the more difficult ones.[41]

Correct timing is often a matter of making the most of available opportunities. Police management should be ready to take advantage of any opportunity that could champion the cause of community policing.

> Those opportunities can be defined as events that throw the spotlight on police policy and provide a 'case in point' justification for a reform proposal. Ironically, opportunities often come disguised as crises, and managers must resist the instinctive impulse to think first of damage control. Managers interested in reform will embrace crises and make the most of them... . [42]

Managing Internal Change

Community policing necessitates the introduction of fundamental and comprehensive change to the police agency. Organizational efforts must support the evolving responsibilities of patrol officers. For example, information systems should move beyond the efficient processing of criminal offense reports to the delivery of timely and accurate information to officers. Training will govern the pace of change and should affect more than just the new recruits. Performance evaluation should no longer be a mere feedback mechanism, but instead should be a tool to facilitate the change process. Successful implementation of community policing entails careful examination of the following organizational issues.

Deployment of Personnel

Permanent or long-term shifts and beat assignments must be instituted if patrol officers are to form lasting and productive partnerships with the community. Community policing depends on this stability. In addition, community boundaries should be carefully drawn to preserve the integrity of existing neighborhoods and to encourage cooperation within the community.

A comprehensive analysis of workloads across shifts and areas is essential to guide the deployment of personnel. This analysis should include data for each community covering the following areas:

n The frequency and nature of calls for service.

n The frequency and nature of criminal activity.

---

41. Wycoff, Mary Ann and Timothy Oettmeier. Forthcoming. 1994.

42. Sherman, Lawrence W. and Anthony V. Bouza in Gary W. Cordner, Craig B. Fraser, and Chuck Wexler. "Research, Planning and Implementation." Local Government Police Management, ed. William A. Geller. Washington, D.C.: International City Management Association, 3d edition. 1991:sidebar.

n The expectations for response time.

n The estimated time needed for community partnership and problem-solving activities.

Some agencies will need to increase the number of officers who are assigned to patrol operations and to readjust existing patrol assignments. Criminal investigation units may need to be surveyed to determine if efforts are being duplicated, which could allow some officers to return to patrol. Civilians could also be hired for support positions not requiring policing skills, in order to reassign police personnel to community patrols.

Supervision

Consistent supervision is necessary for effective community policing. Supervision will suffer if sergeants or lieutenants have schedules that only partially overlap those of the patrol officers. Close collaboration between patrol officers and their supervisors is as critical to successful community policing as the partnership between the officer and the community members.

Close collaboration between patrol officers and their supervisors is as critical to successful community policing as the partnership between the officer and the community members.

While patrol officers need consistent supervision, "The attitude that police officers must be guided and directed at every turn must be discarded.... " [43] Supervisors should function as mentors, motivators, and facilitators. Community policing's broad approach to problem solving can enhance communication and interaction between departmental levels. If middle managers are made an integral part of the problem-solving process, they will become another resource for patrol officers, rather than just another level of supervision.[44] By acting as liaisons, running interference, and suggesting appropriate auxiliary support, supervisors can help patrol officers respond to a wide variety of service demands.

Among the community policing responsibilities for first-line supervisors and mid-level managers are the following:

n Maintaining beat integrity.

n Overseeing the creation of beat profiles.

n Working with officers and community residents to create a system for the allocation and utilization of resources.

n Working with officers and community members to develop, implement, and manage problem-solving systems.

43. Oettmeier, Timothy N., and William H. Bieck. Integrating Investigative Operations Through Neighborhood-Oriented Policing: Executive Session #2. Houston: Houston Police Department. 1988:p.35.

44. Sparrow, Malcolm K. Implementing Community Policing. Perspectives on Policing. Washington, D.C.: National Institute of Justice and John F. Kennedy School of Government, Harvard University. 1988:p.6.

n Assessing results and providing feedback on accomplishments and progress made in addressing problems of crime and disorder.

Supervisors should also bring patrol officers into the management process, facilitate group cohesiveness, and assist personnel in reaching their maximum potential.

Mid-level managers should eliminate impediments to the process of problem solving and to the attainment of results. They must learn to manage multi-functional teams and to assume more responsibility for strategic planning, as well as become actively involved in mobilizing the community in crime-prevention activities.

Mid-level managers should conduct regular meetings with their staff to discuss plans, activities, and results. They should evaluate the progress or failure of strategies, programs, or responses based on performance indicators supplied by officers, supervisors, and community members. Managers have a responsibility to enrich the jobs of their personnel by delegating authority, acting as mentors, and overseeing training and education. They also must meet frequently with their superiors to provide updates, seek direction and guidance, and help expand strategies to address crime and disorder within communities.

Human Resource Development

Training is key to the effective implementation of community policing. Training should communicate and reinforce the changes taking place in organizational values and policies, and should help build consensus, resolve, and unity both inside and outside the police organization.

Community policing skills should be integrated into the training curricula, not treated as a separate component of the training program. Training in community policing should supplement law enforcement techniques with communication and leadership skills that will encourage participation from the community. All personnel must become skilled in the techniques of problem solving, motivating, and team-building. Training should involve the entire agency and should include civilian personnel who can enlist participation in community meetings, help the police organization sharpen its marketing message, and incorporate sophisticated technology into the organization's service-oriented operations.

Initial training efforts should be directed at managers and supervisors, who may feel their authority is being eroded by the modified priorities of the organization.[45] More important, they must be relied on to transmit and translate the new concepts to those they supervise.

---

45. Oettmeier, Timothy N., and William H. Bieck. Integrating Investigative Operations Through Neighborhood-Oriented Policing: Executive Session #2. Houston: Houston Police Department. 1988.

The training of mid-level managers should emphasize their role in facilitating the problem-solving process by coaching, coordinating, and evaluating the efforts of patrol officers. To prepare mid-level managers for their community policing responsibilities, one agency chief required all personnel with the rank of sergeant and above to attend training sessions that had three goals: to show supervisors how to manage officers' time so that problems could be addressed without diminishing police capability for handling calls, to describe how problems should be analyzed, and to ensure that all trainees knew what was expected of them and their officers.[46]

Patrol officers must also receive extensive training that encourages and develops both initiative and discretionary ability—a dramatic departure from traditional thinking. They must develop planning, organization, problem solving, communication, and leadership skills through ongoing, thorough training. Eventually, these officers will be able to assist in the training of others.

Systems for evaluating personnel performance should reflect the goals of community policing.

Performance Evaluation and Reward

Performance evaluation can be a valuable management tool for facilitating change and can help communicate agency priorities to employees.

Systems for evaluating personnel performance should reflect the goals of community policing. "Emphasizing quality over quantity represents a major difference between traditional policing and community-oriented policing."[47] Patrol officers could be evaluated on how well they know their beats—a prerequisite for identification of problems—and how effectively they and their supervisors have adopted problem-solving techniques. Other relevant performance measures include the extent to which personnel have formed partnerships with the community and the nature of their contributions to this team effort. Since officers are working as part of a team, they should not be evaluated as if they were operating alone.

The occasional mistake made by an officer seeking to solve community issues in a proactive manner would be an inappropriate measure of performance. "Managers cannot have it both ways. They cannot ask officers to be risk-takers and then discipline them when occasional mistakes occur."[48] The insight, initiative, and creativity shown by personnel should be considered in the performance appraisal; the motivation behind the action also must be

---

46. Eck, John E., and William Spelman. *Problem Solving: Problem-Oriented Policing in Newport News.* Washington, D.C.: Police Executive Research Forum. 1987:pp.104–6.

47. Brann, Joseph E., and Suzanne Whalley. "COPPS: The Transformation of Police Organizations." *Community-Oriented Policing and Problem Solving.* Sacramento: Attorney General's Crime Prevention Center. 1992:p.74.

48. Kelling, George L., Robert Wasserman, Hubert Williams. *Police Accountability and Community Policing.* Washington, D.C.: National Institute of Justice and John F. Kennedy School of Government, Harvard University. 1988:p.6.

considered. Mistakes made in an honest attempt to solve a problem should not be evaluated in the same manner as mistakes made through carelessness, lack of commitment, or deliberate disregard for policing policies.

Retaining the services of personnel who are skilled in community policing depends, in large part, on appropriate rewards for solid performance. Rewards must be consistent with the values and methods associated with community policing. Patrol officers and supervisors should be evaluated and rewarded for exceptional skills in problem solving or community mobilization efforts, rather than on the number of calls handled or parking tickets issued.

Rewards also include the establishment of well-defined and suitable career paths for all personnel. Specific career development opportunities should reward past effort and allow room for growth, especially for patrol officers. The backbone of community policing is the patrol officer and the status, pay, and working conditions of this position should encourage people to spend an entire career in patrol. "In effect, what is needed is a system that rewards advancement through skill levels in the same job as much or more than it rewards advancement through the ranks."[49]

Management should also consider expanding the criteria for the existing award program and placing more emphasis on community partnership and problem-solving skills. Some departments have invited community members to help select police award recipients. Others have added awards for community members who participate in police efforts. These awards will help solidify commitments and encourage continued cooperation among community policing participants.

Workload Control and Information Systems

The efficient management of service calls is essential for officers to have sufficient time to interact and work with community members to solve problems of crime and disorder. Most agencies control 911 calls for service by determining which calls demand an immediate response and which can be handled with alternate responses or through a referral to another agency. Nonemergency calls can be handled by delayed officer response, by telephone, by mail, or by having the caller come to the station. Research shows that the public will not insist on an immediate response to a nonemergency service request if the alternative response is both appropriate and performed as described.[50]

---

49. Moore, Mark H., and Darrel W. Stephens. Beyond Command and Control: The Strategic Management of Police Departments. Washington, D.C.: Police Executive Research Forum. 1991:p.94.

50. Eck, John E., and William Spelman. "A Problem-Oriented Approach to Police Service Delivery." Police and Policing: Contemporary Issues, ed. Dennis Jay Kenney. New York: Praeger. 1989:p.101.

The problem-solving orientation of community policing requires a greater emphasis on analytic skills and expert systems management to obtain the most valuable information support. Information support will have to be provided for problems that have not been previously studied and for the incorporation of data from outside the department.[51] Analysis must go beyond identifying and forecasting crime patterns; tactical analysis should be supplemented with strategic analysis.

> ...strategic analysis seeks to identify factors that contribute to crime and non-crime problems. Strategic analysis is a natural by-product of the problem-oriented approach ....Strategic analysts should attempt to identify why problems exist in neighborhoods as well as identify the conditions that contribute to and perpetuate crime. This information will certainly prove useful in the planning and implementation of tactical responses and crime prevention strategies.[52]

Strategic analysis will require that information be collected by a number of unconventional methods, e.g., conducting neighborhood victimization surveys, canvassing rehabilitation centers and hospitals, interacting with school officials, and assessing the impact of environmental changes on criminal activity.

Technology tends to heighten the isolation of the police from the public; therefore, management must ensure that technological innovations are integrated into community policing activities in a way that fosters meaningful cooperation and aids in the process of problem solving.

Modern CAD (computer-aided dispatch) systems can assist in prioritizing police response to service requests. Cellular telephones, pagers, fax machines, and voice mail can also relieve the overburdened 911 systems and provide vital communication links between communities and the police. In addition, geocoding and mapping technology can prove invaluable to the problem-solving process.

> Advancements in technology now allow computerized maps of neighbor-hood activity. [In a test] using personal computers with specially designed software, community groups were able to map data provided by daily police reports... .This strategy holds considerable promise for mapping less-serious incivilities (not only the dramatic incidents) that lower the quality of neighborhood life... .Research suggests that releasing local crime statistics to the public will not increase the public's

Analysis must go beyond identifying and forecasting crime patterns; tactical analysis should be supplemented with strategic analysis.

51. Sparrow, Malcolm. Information Systems and the Development of Policing. Perspectives on Policing. Washington, D.C.: National Institute of Justice and John F. Kennedy School of Government, Harvard University. 1993:p.4.

52. Oettmeier, Timothy N., and William H. Bieck. Integrating Investigative Operations Through Neighborhood-Oriented Policing. Executive Session #2. Houston: Houston Police Department. 1988:p.64.

fear of crime so long as the statistics are accompanied by specific, feasible crime prevention recommendations.[53]

All data should be made available through an integrated management information system that can be conveniently accessed by patrol officers, supervisors, command staff, and support personnel. This might entail the use of laptop computers and other mobile communications equipment. Wide dissemination and information sharing are essential components of community policing. Pertinent and appropriate information should be made available to members of the community whenever possible. For example, statistics showing an increase in burglaries or rapes in a specific section of town should be shared with the community to further the problem-solving process.

Facilities

Effective community collaboration and interaction will require patrol officers to be more accessible to community members. "Storefront" police offices or "mini-stations" within neighborhoods can be established quite inexpensively, particularly with assistance from the community. The duties of staffing storefront facilities can be shared among officers, civilian employees, and community residents. These sites provide officers and citizens with the opportunity to discuss problems and plan activities. One police jurisdiction operated a storefront station at a shopping mall, while another used a closed-down roadhouse in a rural area to provide residents with easier access to police services. Some deputies in sparsely populated rural areas are allowed to report in by phone, instead of driving many miles to attend roll call, so that contact with community residents can be maximized. In a sense, the deputies' homes become satellite stations, allowing them greater access to the community.

Facilitating the Implementation Process

Astute chief executives will realize that leadership ability can be found at many levels, both inside and outside the police organization. They should enlist the help of people whose ideas, drive, and ability will help spur the progress of community policing. However, police executives must take responsibility for directing implementation efforts and outlining the parameters for addressing the various facets of community policing. Strong and continued leadership from the top of the organization will reduce confusion and disagreement at lower levels.

Police chiefs will not be able to manage the entire implementation process; therefore, a team or committee, one or more internal coordinators, and outside sources such as consultants should be designated by the chief.

53. Rosenbaum, Dennis P., Eusevio Hernandez, and Sylvester Daughtry, Jr. "Crime Prevention, Fear Reduction, and the Community." Local Government Police Management, ed. William A. Geller. Washington, D.C.: International City Management Association. 1991:p.116.

Members of an implementation team, task force, or committee will also have other responsibilities; therefore, an internal coordinator may be needed to provide daily support for team efforts. For greater effectiveness, internal coordinators should be recruited from the command level of the organization to avoid communication problems.

Outside consultants can also facilitate implementation because they are frequently able to gain access to all levels of the organization more easily than an internal coordinator. Consultants can bring a wealth of experience to the implementation process, including knowledge about the implementation of community policing strategies and suggestions for gathering relevant information. Occasionally consultants may encounter resistance within agencies that are not accustomed to external assistance. Executives loaned from private sector companies also may be useful to police organizations. "The private sector uses such programs to allow one or more employees to work, with pay, for a not-for-profit or community organization for as long as a year at a time."[54]

. . . top management should consider creating a broad-based implementation team.

To ensure a smooth transition to community policing, top management should consider creating a broad-based implementation team. An agencywide team, which could be divided into a number of committees, should adequately represent all levels of the agency in experience and function. An even broader team might include representatives from local government, police unions, other agencies, and members of the community whose assistance would be instrumental to the success of a community policing strategy.

Officers on the implementation team must be allowed to participate outside the traditional lines of authority.[55] This means that while a chairperson will direct and coordinate each committee's activities, there should be no rank within committees. The police chief must have frequent contact with all committees. In addition, the efforts of committees should be coordinated by one or more facilitators who share the chief's thinking and understand the ultimate goals of community policing.

Marketing: Selecting a Message and an Image

Before implementing a community policing strategy, the agency should communicate the concept of community policing to its own personnel and to the community, including political and business leaders and the media. Different emphases and images may be appropriate for different audiences; however, a message to one group should not contradict or neutralize an equally valid message to another.

54. Williams, Hubert. "External Resources." Local Government Police Management, ed. William A. Geller. Washington, D.C.: International City Management Association. 1991:p.465.

55. Wadman, Robert C., and Robert K. Olson. Community Wellness: A New Theory of Policing. Washington, D.C.: Police Executive Research Forum. 1990:p.61.

For example, messages to officers focusing on problem solving and arrests might conflict with images directed at the general public showing officers distributing teddy bears to preschoolers. Both messages and roles are valid; one emphasizes problem solving as a valuable anticrime tool, while the other shows the benefits of trust-building and partnerships with the community.

Media involvement ensures a wide dissemination of the community policing message and encourages the media to stay involved in future community policing efforts . . . .

To avoid sending contradictory messages, agencies should settle on a dominant theme and communicate it consistently both internally and externally. For example, the theme might emphasize a new "customer-service" orientation to policing, focus on partnership building, or highlight the prospects community policing holds for creating secure neighborhoods. Subsidiary points—problem solving, community contact, or ridding neighborhoods of signs of neglect or disorder—could be grouped under the umbrella of this central theme. An excellent example of a central theme is the "Together We Can" slogan that will steer the marketing of community policing efforts in Chicago.

Marketing involves communicating through symbols, stories about real-life situations, and testimonials by those whom the community and officers respect. Marketing messages are conveyed internally through memos, roll-call briefings, newsletters, and special videos, and in person by command staff and chief executives, among others. Externally, they are publicized through public forums, posters, flyers, meetings, public service announcements, and the officers' personal contact with community members.

Although the use of a label or acronym to help market community policing seems a small matter, it needs careful consideration.

> If employees are generally supportive of the change, then the label provides a positive rallying symbol ....If, on the other hand, there is substantial resistance to the change, then the label becomes a negative rallying symbol ....People begin to play games with the acronym. Neighborhood-Oriented Policing becomes 'Nobody On Patrol' or 'NOPE.'"[56]

The media must be included early in the implementation process to market successfully the idea of community policing. Media involvement ensures a wide dissemination of the community policing message and encourages the media to stay involved in future community policing efforts; the media also will be less apt to "derail" if there is a bump in the crime statistics or if some community policing policies are less effective than hoped. If the budget allows, media consultants can be useful. The agency's internal media relations unit should thoroughly understand the chief executive's vision of community policing and communicate it clearly in news releases and interviews. All who are marketing the concept must be careful not to claim more for community policing than it can deliver.

---

56. Wycoff, Mary Ann and Timothy Oettmeier. Forthcoming. 1994.

Assessing the Progress of Community Policing

A critical aspect of implementation is the assessment of community policing efforts, both in terms of achieving necessary change within the organization itself and accomplishing external goals (such as, establishing working relationships with the community and reducing levels of crime, fear, and disorder). Ongoing assessment meets a number of fundamental needs.

Every government and public agency, including the police, should be able to give an accurate account of its current activities to policymakers and taxpayers. Thus, ongoing assessment of policy and performance should be a primary function of any policing organization. Assessment becomes even more vital when an organization is undergoing the comprehensive changes that a shift to community policing will entail. Constant assessment of the process of change is needed for managers to determine how to keep the implementation process on track. The most effective strategies also need to be identified so managers can make informed choices about where to allocate limited resources.

Ongoing assessment helps give the organization a clear sense of direction and allows management to focus efforts on the most productive and efficient practices. Therefore, assessment is indispensable in determining which elements of community policing should be maintained, altered, or eliminated, and offers key decisionmakers in the jurisdiction a way to gauge the impact and cost-effectiveness of community policing efforts.

Assessment will help determine whether necessary changes in the support systems are taking place and whether appropriate efforts are being made to accomplish the stated goals. Assessment also can help communicate agency expectations to employees.

Giving community members a way to measure the success of community policing efforts is critical to maintaining strong ties, ensuring continued participation, and documenting the progress made. Conversely, evaluations of the community policing strategy from government and community leaders will affect how future cooperative efforts are constructed. Thorough assessment helps make police more responsive to the community's needs, which should strengthen the trust and partnership on which community policing is based.

Developing a sound assessment program should begin with a strategic plan that outlines the goals, methods, objectives, and timetables, and assigns personnel for internal and external changes. These goals and responsibilities will form the basis of performance assessment and will allow police leadership to detect failures and roadblocks, as well as to chart progress and document accomplishments.

Assessing Internal Changes

Large gaps can exist between policy and actions, therefore, management must take nothing for granted in the implementation of community policing policies and procedures. The chief executive should constantly ask, "How is the implementation going? Is it on track? What problems are occurring? What help is needed?"

In smaller organizations, these questions can be answered through a process called "management by walking around" in which the chief visits key managers and implementation groups to get on-the-spot reports on implementation efforts. The chief should also consult patrol officers to obtain their views on the implementation process. In every organization, the chief executive should hold regular meetings with the personnel responsible for overseeing community policing implementation and should ask for reports on efforts with the goal of both reinforcing accountability and allowing for immediate discussion of problems. Regular reports on progress and problems relating to specific community policing objectives and timetables should be supplied by members of the implementation team.

Assessment of the more intangible internal changes, for example, the decentralization of management, can be complex. The chief executive and the head of the implementation team could meet regularly with groups of managers and supervisors to discuss changes in decisionmaking authority. Periodic personnel surveys can also help determine what modifications have occurred in management style, which obstacles stand in the way of change, and how agency leadership can facilitate the necessary adjustments in the roles of managers, supervisors, and patrol officers.

Three Criteria for Assessment

Evaluating the impact of community policing is critical for many reasons. Key decisionmakers must be able to judge the strategy's impact and cost-effectiveness, and the police organization must be able to measure the success or failure of its policies and activities. As with implementation methods, assessment measures will vary depending on the size of the organization and the nature of its current policies. Ongoing monitoring will expedite the implementation process, attract support, aid problem solving, and reveal new opportunities for productive partnerships with the community.

In the past, police efforts usually have been evaluated on a traditional and narrow set of criteria (e.g., crime statistics, the number of 911 calls, the length of police response, the number of arrests and citations, etc.). These assessments were often taken only at times of serious crime increases.

Many of the traditional methods of assessment remain valid, but can measure only the effectiveness of crime-fighting tactics and cannot gauge the effect of crime-prevention efforts. Changes in the scope of policing necessitate a revised system for evaluating the performance of individuals, as well as agencies. As police take a proactive role in deterring crime, a broader set of assessment criteria, which incorporate traditional measures of crime-fighting activities with those that encompass community partnership and problem-solving activities, will be needed.

Creativity, initiative, and ingenuity should be emphasized in the evaluation of individual officers.

Traditional crime-control activities should become only one of the ways in which the community policing strategy and individual officers are assessed. Many indications of the success of community policing efforts are intangible (e.g., absence of fear, quality of interaction with community members, etc.); therefore, assessing a community policing strategy is a qualitative as well as a quantitative process. The values that the department promotes will form the basis of sound qualitative measures of effectiveness. Assessment should reward organizational and individual behavior that assists in deterring crime and solving other neighborhood problems. Creativity, initiative, and ingenuity should be emphasized in the evaluation of individual officers. Three major criteria—effectiveness, efficiency, and equity—can be used to provide the quantitative and qualitative measures needed to assess the success of a community policing strategy.

Effectiveness

An effective community policing strategy will reduce neighborhood crime, decrease citizens' fear of crime, and enhance the quality of life in the community. An important goal of community policing is to provide higher quality service to neighborhoods; therefore, customer satisfaction becomes an important measure of effectiveness. The perception of progress among community members and ongoing feedback from all elements of the community are essential parts of the assessment process. Randomly and routinely conducted surveys will inform the agency of the public view of police performance, the level of fear and concern, and will make the agency aware of the extent to which community members feel as if they are participants in the community policing effort.

One of the core components of community policing is community partnership. Therefore, an early measure of effectiveness will be the number and type of community partnerships that have been formed. The cooperation and participation of community members is necessary to deter crime and reduce the fear of crime in the neighborhood. Assessing the effectiveness of community policing efforts includes determining whether problems have been solved and judging how well the managers and patrol officers have applied the community partnership and problem-solving components of community policing described in Chapter 3.

Assessment should measure whether a problem was solved and how this was accomplished. As stated earlier, the number of arrests made is only one possible measure of effective problem solving; solving problems often does not involve arrest and, in many cases, does not guarantee that a problem will disappear completely. For example, the officer (cited in Chapter 3), who determined that one of the underlying causes of an increase in convenience store robberies was that cash registers could not be seen by passersby, did not eradicate the burglary. However, his efforts did provide valuable information that could help deter future robberies. Satisfactory assessment measures for community policing must give proper credit to officers like this who successfully abate a problem through means other than arrest. The officer's contribution to solving the problem and his consultations with members of the community showed the concern and effectiveness of police officers and created the goodwill for the department that is crucial to the success of community policing.

The number and type of problems solved and the creativity and scope of the solutions will provide a way to measure community policing's effectiveness. Not all of the problems will involve criminal activity, and many will not even be considered a priority by the police agency. However, where serious crime is not involved, the concerns and fears of community members should order the priorities of the agency.

In community policing, officers may act as facilitators to mobilize community support. They may also function as mediators in disputes between individuals or organizations, or take responsibility for referring a problem to the appropriate social or government agency. The effective use of government and community agencies in problem solving is an indication that community policing policies are working. Thus, the mobilization and intelligent use of community resources in solving problems and the sensitive handling of dissension become important factors in assessing the performance of officers and the success of the program.

Increased levels of community participation in crime reduction and prevention efforts is another indication of program success. Community members will not act if they are afraid or suspicious. Community members should become more willing to work with the police in a variety of ways, ranging from converting abandoned buildings to community assets to involving police actively in neighborhood watch groups. They might also be more comfortable providing information on criminal activity in the area. In fact, calls to report crime may increase considerably during the early phases of community policing implementation, as community confidence in police capability rises and community trust increases. However, the number of 911 calls will likely decrease over time, which will provide a quantitative measure of the strategy's effect. For instance, emergency calls in the pioneering Flint,

Assessment should measure whether a problem was solved and how this was accomplished.

Michigan, foot patrol district dropped 43 percent over the course of the experiment.[57]

A concrete indication of community policing's success is the commitment of an increased level of community resources devoted to crime reduction efforts. Active consultation and financial participation by public and private agencies, schools, and the business community will demonstrate that community-partnership efforts are working. Communities also should begin to initiate and conduct projects with minimal guidance from the police.

Renewed activity within the community also will demonstrate the effectiveness of community policing efforts, particularly in areas where citizens have been afraid to leave their homes. Reduction in fear can also result in the perception among residents that crime is on the wane, whether or not this is statistically accurate. An increased willingness of citizens to walk to schools and parks, patronize stores, and go to restaurants and movies will signal a general decrease in fear of crime. In turn, the very fact that community members are reclaiming their streets will help deter future criminal activity and create more vigorous neighborhoods.

Improved quality of life is difficult to measure but is an important goal of community policing and will be reflected in comments from community members. Ridding the streets of gangs, drunks, panhandlers, and prostitutes—perhaps with the help of public and private social agencies—will enhance the quality of life. Removing signs of neglect (e.g., abandoned cars, derelict buildings, and garbage and debris) will offer tangible evidence that community policing efforts are working to bring about increased order in the community.

In community policing, the police function includes the provision of services that in the recent past have been regarded as outside policing's purview. These services include aiding accident and crime victims, arbitrating neighborhood and domestic disputes, and providing emergency medical and social services. An analysis of the nature of calls for police service (e.g., a lower percentage of calls reporting criminal activity in proportion to calls requesting social assistance) will provide a measure of how well the strategy is working.

Renewed activity within the community will demonstrate the effectiveness of community policing efforts, particularly in areas where citizens have been afraid to leave their homes.

Efficiency

Efficiency means getting the most results with available resources. To measure the efficiency of community policing, the resources of the police agency, local government and private agencies, citizen groups, the business community, and the neighborhood must first be defined. The assessment must then determine whether these resources are being used to their fullest to solve any given problem. Agencies that can successfully enhance and realign their resources by forming community partnerships will be able to make community policing more efficient and cost-effective.

---

57. Trojanowicz, Robert C. "An Evaluation of a Neighborhood Foot Patrol Program." Journal of Police Science and Administration 11(1983):p.417.

Two major shifts must occur within the police organization if community policing is to work efficiently. Staunch partnerships and collaborative efforts must first be established with the community. The command structure of the police organization must then be decentralized so that problem solving, decisionmaking, and accountability are spread to all levels of the organization. Such decentralization challenges personnel to be more creative and more effective because the decisions they make are more timely and influenced by firsthand knowledge of the facts.[58] Decentralization also gives higher level managers more time to formulate strategies that will improve the organization's performance.

In a decentralized policing organization, neighborhood patrol officers are responsible for the daily policing needs of the community, with guidance and backing from supervisors. Their long-term shifts and neighborhood patrol assignments give them the opportunity to function more efficiently and successfully.

Patrol officers who handle daily police functions can form stronger bonds with the community. This "pride of ownership" motivates both parties to solve the problems that affect the security and harmony of the neighborhood. Patrol officers will experience greater job satisfaction as they accept higher levels of responsibility and accountability. Officers are often able to resolve issues quickly, allowing them to see the immediate results of their efforts.

With high morale and greater job satisfaction, patrol officers will more effectively mobilize the community. If they are highly motivated, given the necessary support, and appropriately rewarded for their efforts, the job satisfaction they experience will help make the community policing strategy a success.

The roles and responsibilities of all personnel in the police organization are altered so that the leadership and ingenuity officers display will become important factors in determining the efficiency of the program. Assessment and reward procedures must therefore be revised accordingly.

Community help will increase the efficiency of the program and relieve some of the strain of tight police budgets. Partnerships in the community can bring fresh resources to problems, even those traditionally considered "police-only" business. According to one sheriff, "There is virtually no limitation on how much more effective and efficient a sheriff's office can become, working collectively as a partner with community members while, at the same time, saving resources, dollars, and frustration on the part of constituents."[59]

---

58. Moore, Mark H., and Darrel W. Stephens. Beyond Command and Control: The Strategic Management of Police Departments. Washington, D.C.: Police Executive Research Forum. 1991:p.76.

59. Prinslow, Robert J. "Community Policing in Marion County, Oregon." Roll Call. Special edition (June 1993):p.9.

Decentralized decisionmaking and community partnership engenders new organizational and resource issues that must be addressed to operate the system efficiently. Budgets must reflect the goals of community policing by allocating money and resources in proportion to the results achieved. With decentralization police officers who have the greatest responsibility for the daily policing operations will have more direct input into budgetary decisions and greater accountability for financial decisions, actions taken, and results achieved.

Efficiency must be built into each aspect of the community policing strategy—from the creation of community boundaries that cultivate productive alliances to the adoption of technologies that increase communication. Expanded and thorough training is paramount in an efficient shift to community policing. Intensive training, although initially costly in terms of dollars and time, will eventually make the process more efficient, as well-trained and experienced personnel share practical knowledge with colleagues.

Efficiency in larger agencies may be increased by redefining job functions at all management levels. For example, one large jurisdiction implementing community policing required sergeants to coordinate officer decisionmaking across beats as necessary and to confer with their lieutenants on decisions that involved a large or long-term commitment of resources. Lieutenants in turn apprised their respective captains about happenings on beats across their districts. Such amended roles for midlevel managers may promote efficiency through fewer levels of supervision. While an important supervisory role is to help maximize the amount of time neighborhood officers can spend in their communities, community policing will require supervisors to coordinate problem-solving activities within and across communities, help secure resources, evaluate activities and decisions, and provide guidance and support to neighborhood officers.

Also central to achieving efficiency in time and dollars is controlling calls for service. Sophisticated technological advances can help prioritize calls and facilitate communication among community policing partners. Alternative response strategies for nonemergency calls include a delayed-officer response and officer response by appointment. Low-priority situations can be handled by telephone, walk-in, and mail-in reporting. "All indications are that these systems save an enormous amount of time, reduce officer frustration, and are equally satisfactory to the callers."[60]

Effectiveness and efficiency are important yardsticks by which to measure community policing's achievements, but equity, the third major criterion for judging progress, has the greatest impact on the success of community policing.

Effectiveness and efficiency are important yardsticks by which to measure community policing's achievements, but equity has the greatest impact on the success of community policing.

---

60. Goldstein, Herman. *Problem-Oriented Policing.* New York: McGraw Hill. 1990: pp.20–21.

Equity

Equity is grounded firmly in the Constitution of the United States, which all police officers are sworn to uphold. A foremost tenet of community policing is equity; that is, all citizens should have a say in how they are governed. Officers may relate better to citizens as individuals because they cooperate closely with and are recognized as an integral part of the community. Community policing can thus become a force for enhancing democratic principles.

Community policing provides an opportunity to emphasize uncompromising integrity, unyielding standards of fairness, and unwavering equality because officers have to work closely with the community and will be increasingly confronted with ethical dilemmas.

Equity, as understood in community policing activities, has three dimensions: equal access to police services by all citizens, equal treatment of all individuals under the U.S. Constitution, and equal distribution of police services and resources among communities.

Equal access to police services. All citizens, regardless of race, religion, personal characteristics, or group affiliation, must have equal access to police services for a full and productive partnership with a community. The paramount commitment of community policing should be respect for all citizens and sensitivity to their needs. Neighborhood officers must not discriminate against any community members. Supervisors should help ensure that police services are readily available throughout the community.

In addition, lines of communication must be kept open with all partners in the community policing effort. Favoritism of one group over another will severely hamper future cooperative efforts. Groups who are more vocal than others cannot be permitted to use community policing to serve their own purposes. Police must prevent such behavior before it adversely affects the trust that has been established within and among communities.

Equal treatment under the constitution. Police must treat all individuals according to the constitutional rights that officers are sworn to protect and enforce. Careful attention to the constitutional rights of citizens, victims, or perpetrators will help to engender bonds of trust between the police and community. Police must treat all persons with respect and impartiality—including the homeless, the poor, and the mentally or physically handicapped. They must reject stereotypes, ignore skin color, and use reason and persuasion rather than coercion wherever possible because inequitable or harsh treatment can lead to frustration, hostility, and even violence within a community. Such unethical behavior will imperil the trust so necessary to community policing.

Some contemporary community activists and leaders have experienced past confrontations with the police which may present serious challenges to implementing community policing and involving the community in policing efforts.

Equal distribution of police services and resources among communities. Because community policing customizes policing services to the needs of each community, services should be distributed equitably among poor and minority communities. Care must be taken, however, to ensure that this is the case.

For equitable distribution of resources among communities, each community must articulate its needs and be willing to work with the police to ensure its share of police services. Each neighborhood officer must listen to the community members, and be willing to work with the community members to meet those needs. Poor and minority neighborhoods can present particular challenges for some patrol officers, who may have to bridge differences of race and class before a level of trust and cooperation can be established.

Some neighborhoods may appear unwilling to help police in their efforts to improve life in the community. Officers must realize that sometimes "the community seems so helpless because it feels abandoned and would discover new strengths if only the police could make an effective alliance with important community elements....Departments that have taken early steps [into community policing] are full of stories of apparently lost neighborhoods that flowered under new police attention."[61]

One community must not be given preference over another; all communities must have equal access to police services. Equity, however, may not always mean equal distribution of police services and resources. Wealthier communities are often able to contribute more resources to the problem-solving process than can poorer communities. Crime rates will also be higher in some communities, requiring more police intervention and a larger share of police resources to decrease crime and transform neighborhoods from places of fear into city or county assets.

. . . all communities must have equal access to police services.

Refining the Assessment Process

Assessment of community policing is an ongoing process that should include a reevaluation of the assessment measures themselves. With more experience in community policing, a police agency will be able to develop measures that accurately chart successes and failures and indicate where changes need to be made.

The values of the policing organization must guide the move to community policing, and shape every decision made and every action taken. Above all, police organizations must be responsive to community priorities and demands for service from the beginning of the community policing effort.

61. Sparrow, Malcolm, Mark H. Moore, and David M. Kennedy. *Beyond 911: A New Era for Policing.* USA: Basic Books. 1990:p.180.

Conclusion

Police agencies should not allow political leaders and the public to develop unrealistic expectations for community policing in terms of crime deterrence or speed of implementation. Community policing calls for long-term commitment; it is not a quick fix. Achieving ongoing partnerships with the community and eradicating the underlying causes of crime will take planning, flexibility, time, and patience. Management can measure progress by their success in meeting interim goals and must reinforce the concept inside and outside the organization that success is reached through a series of gradual improvements.

Local political leadership may be eager for fast results, but police leadership must make it clear to city and county officials that implementing community policing is an incremental and long-term process. Political and community leaders must be regularly informed of the progress of community policing efforts to keep them interested and involved. The police organization, from the chief executive down, must stress that the success of community policing depends on sustained joint efforts of the police, local government, public and private agencies, and members of the community. This cooperation is indispensable to deterring crime and revitalizing our neighborhoods.

Bibliography

Advisory Commission on Intergovernmental Relations. *The New Grass Roots Government.* Washington, D.C.: U.S. Government Printing Office. 1972.

Advisory Commission on Intergovernmental Relations. *State-Local Relations in the Criminal Justice System.* Washington, D.C.: U.S. Government Printing Office. 1971.

Allevato, S. *Developing of a Law Enforcement Plan for California Cities Committed to Quality Service Through Community-Oriented Policing.* Sacramento: California Commission on Peace Officer Standards and Training. 1989.

American Association of Retired Persons Criminal Justice Services Program Department. *Neighborhood Watch—Communities Combat Crime.* Washington, D.C.: American Association of Retired Persons. 1983.

Banas, Dennis, and Robert C. Trojanowicz. *Uniform Crime Reporting and Community Policing—An Historical Perspective.* East Lansing, Mich.: National Neighborhood Foot Patrol Center, Michigan State University, School of Criminal Justice. 1985.

Bayley, David H. *The Best Defense.* Washington, D.C.: Police Executive Research Forum. 1992.

Bayley, David H. *Model of Community Policing: The Singapore Story.* Washington, D.C.: U.S. Department of Justice, Office of Justice Programs, National Institute of Justice. 1989.

Behan, Cornelius J. "Responding to Change and Managing Crimewarps." *American Journal of Police* 9(3)(1990).

Belknap, J., Merry Morash, and Robert C. Trojanowicz. *Implementing a Community Policing Model for Work With Juveniles—An Exploratory Study.* East Lansing, Mich.: National Neighborhood Foot Patrol Center, Michigan State University, School of Criminal Justice. 1986.

Bittner, Egon. *Aspects of Police Work.* Boston: Northeastern University Press. 1990.

Blumstein, Alfred, and Jacqueline Cohen. *Criminal Careers and Career Criminals.* Washington, D.C.: National Academy of Sciences. 1986.

Blumstein, Alfred, Jacqueline Cohen, and Daniel Nagin. *Deterrence and Incapacitation: Estimating the Effects of Criminal Sanctions on Crime Rates.* Washington, D.C.: National Academy of Sciences. 1978.

Bowman, Gary W., Simon Hakim, et. al., eds. *Privatizing the United States Justice System: Police, Adjudication, and Corrections Services From the Private Sector.* Jefferson, N.C.: McFarland Company, Inc. 1992.

Boydstun, John E., and Michael E. Sherry. *San Diego Community Profile, Final Report.* Washington, D.C.: Police Foundation. 1975.

Brann, Joseph E., and Suzanne Whalley. "COPPS: The Transformation of Police Organizations." *Community Oriented Policing and Problem Solving.* Sacramento: California Attorney General's Crime Prevention Center. 1992.

Brown, Lee P. "Neighborhood-Oriented Policing." *American Journal of Police Special Issue* 9(3)(1990).

Brown, Lee P. *Community Policing: A Practical Guide for Police Officials.* Perspectives on Policing. Washington, D.C.: U.S. Department of Justice, Office of Justice Programs, National Institute of Justice; and John F. Kennedy School of Government, Harvard University. 1989.

Bureau of Justice Statistics. "Prisoners in 1992." *Bureau of Justice Statistics Bulletin* (May 1992).

Bureau of Justice Statistics. *The Prosecution of Felony Arrests.* Washington, D.C.: U.S. Department of Justice, Office of Justice Programs. 1992.

Bureau of Justice Statistics. "State and Local Police Departments, 1990." *Bureau of Justice Statistics Bulletin* (February 1992).

Bureau of Justice Statistics. *Sourcebook of Criminal Justice Statistics, 1991.* Washington, D.C.: U.S. Department of Justice, Office of Justice Programs. 1992.

Bureau of Justice Statistics. *Criminal Victimization in the United States, 1991.* Washington, D.C.: U.S. Department of Justice, Office of Justice Programs. 1992.

C.F. Productions, Inc. *Crime File: Drugs, Community Response.* Washington, D.C.: U.S. Department of Justice, Office of Justice Programs, National Institute of Justice. 1990.

Chamber of Commerce of the United States. *Marshaling Citizen Power Against Crime.* Washington, D.C. 1970.

Chamber of Commerce of the United States. *Forward Thrust—A Process for Mobilizing Total Community Resources.* Washington, D.C. 1969.

Chamber of Commerce of the United States. *Developing Voluntary Leadership.* Washington, D.C. No Date Given.

Chen, M.M. "System Approach of Needs-Oriented Police Planning: An Empirical Study." *Police Studies* 13(4)(Winter 1990).

Clarke, Ronald V. "Situational Crime Prevention: Its Theoretical Bases and Practical Scope." Crime and Justice: An Annual Review of Research 4(1983).

Community Patrol Officer Program: A Pilot Program in Community Oriented Policing in the 72d Precinct, Interim Progress Report. New York: Vera Institute of Justice. 1984.

Community Policing—Making the Case for Citizen Involvement. Rockville, Md.: Charles Stewart Mott Foundation. 1987.

Cordner, Gary W. "Fear of Crime and the Police—An Evaluation of a Fear-Reduction Strategy." Journal of Police Administration 14(3)(September 1986).

Cordner, Gary W., and Donna C. Hale, eds. What Works in Policing: Operations and Administration Examined. Cincinnati, Ohio: Anderson Publishing Company. 1992.

Couper, David C., and Sabine H. Lobitz. Quality Policing: The Madison Experience. Washington, D.C.: Police Executive Research Forum. 1991.

Cox, S.M. "Policing Into the 21st Century." Police Studies 13(4)(Winter 1990).

Craven, D. Oregon Serious Crime Survey: Attitudes About Crime. Washington, D.C.: U.S. Department of Justice, Office of Justice Programs, National Institute of Justice. 1989.

Criswell, D., and V. King. "Houston's Field Training Practicum." Field Training Quarterly 5(2)(Second Quarter 1988).

Cumming, Elaine, Ian Cumming, and Laural Edell. "Policeman as Philosopher, Guide, and Friend." Social Problems 12(1965).

Daly, N.C., and P.J. Morehead. Evaluation of Community Policing: Final Report of the Community Survey and Police Department Internal Survey. St. Petersburg, Florida: St. Petersburg Police Department. 1992.

Delaware Statistical Analysis Center. East Side Wilmington Anti-Drug Abuse Program Evaluation. Rockville, Md.: U.S. Department of Justice, Office of Justice Programs, National Institute of Justice. 1990.

Donovan, E.J., and W.F. Walsh. "Private Security and Community Policing: Evaluation and Comment." Journal of Criminal Justice. 17(3)(1989).

Dunham, Roger G., and Geoffrey Alpert, eds. Critical Issues in Policing: Contemporary Readings. Prospect Heights, Ill.: Waveland Press Inc. 1989.

Eck, John E., and William Spelman. Problem Solving: Problem-Oriented Policing in Newport News. Washington, D.C.: U.S. Department of Justice, Office of Justice Programs, National Institute of Justice; and Police Executive Research Forum. 1987.

Eck, John E., and William Spelman. "Who Ya Gonna Call? The Police as Problem-Busters." Crime and Delinquency. 33(1987).

Esbensen, F. "Foot Patrol: Of What Value?" American Journal of Police. 6(1) (Spring 1987).

Espinosa, G., and R. Wittmier. "Police Bicycle Patrols: An Integral Part of Community Policing." Campus Enforcement Journal. 21(6) (November–December 1991).

Farmer, Michael T., ed. Differential Police Response Strategies. Washington, D.C.: Police Executive Research Forum. 1981.

Farrell, Michael J. Community Patrol Officer Program: Community-Oriented Policing in New York City Police Department, Interim Progress Report Number 2. New York: Vera Institute of Justice. 1986.

Fleissner, D., N. Feden, E. Scotland, and D. Klinger. Community Policing in Seattle: A Descriptive Study of the South Seattle Crime Reduction Project. Rockville, Md.: U.S. Department of Justice, Office of Justice Programs, National Institute of Justice. 1991.

Freeman, Michael A. "Community-Oriented Policing." MIS Report. International City Management Association. 24(9) (September 1989).

Friedmann, Robert R. "Community Policing: Promises and Challenges." Journal of Contemporary Criminal Justice. 6(2) (May 1990).

Geller, William A., ed. Local Government Police Management. Washington, D.C.: International City Management Association. 1991.

Geller, William A., ed. Police Leadership in America. New York: Praeger Publishers. 1985.

Goldstein, Herman. Problem-Oriented Policing. New York: McGraw Hill, Inc. 1990.

Goldstein, Herman. "Improving Policing: A Problem-Oriented Approach." Crime and Delinquency. 25(1979).

Greene, Jack R. "Foot Patrol and Community Policing: Past Practices and Future Prospects." American Journal of Police. 6(1) (Spring 1987).

Greene, Jack R., and Stephan D. Mastrofski. Community Policing: Rhetoric or Reality. New York: Praeger Publishers. 1988.

Greenwood, Peter W., Jan M. Chaiken, and Joan Petersilia. The Criminal Investigation Process. Lexington: DC Heath. 1977.

Greenwood, Peter W., and Joan Petersilia. The Criminal Investigation Process—Volume I: Summary and Policy Implications. Santa Monica, Calif.: Rand Corporation. 1975.

Gruber, C.A. "Neighborhood Policing." Law Enforcement Technology. 19(5) (May 1992).

Hall, D.L. "Community Policing: An Overview of the Literature." Public Policy Report. 1(1) (June 1990).

Hand, Learned. The Contribution of an Independent Judiciary to Civilization. 1942.

Hansen, K.J. Exploratory Study of the Extension of Local Empowerment Through Community Policing. Washington, D.C.: U.S. Department of Justice, Office of Justice Programs, National Institute of Justice. 1991.

Harrington, Michael. The Other America: Poverty in the United States. New York: Macmillan. 1981.

Hayward Police Department. Community Policing and Problem Solving (COPPS). Hayward: Hayward Police Department. 1991.

Hermanson, S. Police-Community Relations: A Survey Measuring Citizens' Attitudes Towards and Perceptions of the Louisville Police Department. Louisville, Ky.: University of Louisville Urban Studies Center College of Urban and Public Affairs. 1982.

Herzberg, F. "One More Time, How Do You Motivate Employees?" Harvard Business Review (January–February 1968).

Hoover, Larry T., ed. Police Management: Issues and Perspectives. Washington, D.C.: Police Executive Research Forum. 1992.

Independent Commission on the Los Angeles Police Department. Report of the Independent Commission on the Los Angeles Police Department. Los Angeles. 1991.

Institute for Law and Social Research. Expanding the Perspective of Crime Data: Performance Implications for Policymakers. Washington, D.C.: Law Enforcement Assistance Administration. 1977.

International City Management Association. Source Book: Community-Oriented Policing: An Alternative Strategy. Washington, D.C.: U.S. Department of Justice, Office of Justice Programs, National Institute of Justice. 1991.

Jackson, F. Directory of City Policing Programs, Volume 3. Rockville, Md.: U.S. Department of Justice, Office of Justice Programs, National Institute of Justice. 1989.

Jacobs, Jane. The Death and Life of Great American Cities. New York: Vintage. 1961.

Jensen, F.P. Evaluating Police Effectiveness by the Year 2001. Sacramento: California Commission on Peace Officer Standards and Training. 1992.

Johnson, J. Police Officers A to Z. New York: Walker. 1986.

Johnson, M.C. Effectiveness of the Addition of Foot Patrol in Montclair, N.J. Ann Arbor, Mich.: University Microfilms. 1980.

Kansas City Police Department. Response Time Analysis: Volume II—Part I Crime Analysis. Washington, D.C.: U.S. Government Printing Office. 1980.

Kansas City Police Department. *Directed Patrol: A Concept in Community-Specific, Crime-Specific, and Service-Specific Policing.* Kansas City, Mo.: Kansas City Police Department. 1974.

Kelling, George L. *Police and Communities: The Quiet Revolution.* Perspectives on Policing. Washington, D.C.: U.S. Department of Justice, Office of Justice Programs, National Institute of Justice; and John F. Kennedy School of Government, Harvard University. 1988.

Kelling, George L. "Acquiring a Task for Order—The Community and Police." *Crime and Delinquency* 33(1)(January 1987).

Kelling, George L. *Foot Patrol—Crime File Series Study Guide.* Rockville, Md.: U.S. Department of Justice, Office of Justice Programs, National Institute of Justice. 1986.

Kelling, George L. "Conclusions." *The Newark Foot Patrol Experiment.* Washington, D.C.: The Police Foundation. 1981.

Kelling, George L. *Foot Patrol.* Washington, D.C.: U.S. Department of Justice, Office of Justice Programs, National Institute of Justice. 1986.

Kelling, George L., Robert Wasserman, and Hubert Williams. *Police Accountability and Community Policing.* Perspectives on Policing. Washington, D.C.: U.S. Department of Justice, Office of Justice Programs, National Institute of Justice; and John F. Kennedy School of Government, Harvard University. 1988.

Kelling, George L., and Mark H. Moore. *The Evolving Strategy of Policing.* Perspectives on Policing. Washington, D.C.: U.S. Department of Justice, Office of Justice Programs, National Institute of Justice; and John F. Kennedy School of Government, Harvard University. 1988.

Kelling, George L., Anthony Pate, Duane Dieckman, and Charles E. Brown. *The Kansas City Preventive Patrol Experiment: A Technical Report.* Washington, D.C.: Police Foundation. 1974.

Kennedy, David M. *The Strategic Management of Police Resources.* Perspectives on Policing. Washington, D.C.: U.S. Department of Justice, Office of Justice Programs, National Institute of Justice; and John F. Kennedy School of Government, Harvard University. 1993.

Kennedy, L.W. "Evaluation of Community-Based Policing in Canada." *Canadian Police College Journal* 15(4)(1991).

Kenney, Dennis Jay, ed. *Police and Policing: Contemporary Issues.* New York: Praeger Publishers. 1989.

Manning, Peter K. "Community Policing." *American Journal of Police* 3(2)(Spring 1984).

Manual for the Establishment and Operation of a Foot Patrol Program—Books in Brief. Rockville, Md.: National Criminal Justice Reference Service. 1985.

Maryland Department of Public Safety and Correctional Services. *Maryland's Law Enforcement Strategy in Partnership with the People.* Rockville, Md.: National Criminal Justice Reference Service. 1992.

McDonald, P., and Robert Wasserman. *High Performance Police Management: A Source Book.* Rockville, Md.: Police Management Association; and U.S. Department of Justice, Office of Justice Programs, National Institute of Justice. 1988.

McElroy, Jerome E., Colleen A. Cosgrove, and Susan Sadd. *An Examination of the Community Patrol Officer Program (CPOP) in New York City.* New York: Vera Institute of Justice. 1989.

McEwan, Thomas, and John Eck, et al. *Evaluation of Community Crime/ Problem Resolution Through Police Directed Patrol: Executive Summary.* Alexandria, Va.: Institute for Law and Justice; and Washington, D.C.: Police Executive Research Forum. 1989.

McEwan, Thomas, Edward F. Connors III, and Marcia I. Cohen. *Evaluation of the Differential Police Response Field Test.* Washington, D.C.: U.S. Government Printing Office. 1986.

Meese, Edwin III. *Community Policing and the Police Officer.* Perspectives on Policing. Washington, D.C.: U.S. Department of Justice, Office of Justice Programs, National Institute of Justice; and John F. Kennedy School of Government, Harvard University. 1991.

Moore, Mark H., and Darrel W. Stephens. *Beyond Command and Control: The Strategic Management of Police Departments.* Washington, D.C.: Police Executive Research Forum. 1991.

Moore, Mark H. and Robert C. Trojanowicz. *Policing and the Fear of Crime.* Perspectives on Policing. Washington, D.C.: U.S. Department of Justice, Office of Justice Programs, National Institute of Justice; and John F. Kennedy School of Government, Harvard University. 1988.

Moore, Mark H., and Robert C. Trojanowicz. *Corporate Strategies for Policing.* Perspectives on Policing. Washington, D.C.: U.S. Department of Justice, Office of Justice Programs, National Institute of Justice; and John F. Kennedy School of Government, Harvard University. 1988.

Moore, Mark H., Robert C. Trojanowicz, and George L. Kelling. *Crime and Policing.* Perspectives on Policing. Washington, D.C.: U.S. Department of Justice, Office of Justice Programs, National Institute of Justice; and John F. Kennedy School of Government, Harvard University. 1988.

More, Harry W. *Special Topics in Policing.* Cincinnati, Ohio: Anderson Publishing Company. 1992.

Morris, Edward K., and Curtis J. Braukmann, eds. *Behavioral Approaches to Crime and Delinquency: A Handbook of Application, Research, and Concepts.* New York: Plenum Press. 1987.

National Advisory Commission on Civil Disorders. *Report of the National Advisory Commission on Civil Disorders*. Washington, D.C.: U.S. Government Printing Office. 1992.

National Advisory Commission on Criminal Justice Standards and Goals. *Community Crime Prevention*. Washington, D.C.: U.S. Government Printing Office. 1973.

National Institute of Justice. *Community Policing in Seattle: A Model Partnership Between Citizens and Police. Research-in-Brief.* Washington, D.C.: U.S. Department of Justice, Office of Justice Programs. 1992.

Needle, Jerome A., and Raymond T. Galvin. "Community Policing: An Inevitable Progression." *Community Policing: Issues and Options* 1(9)(October 1993).

Newport News Police Department Patrol Division. *COPP (Community Oriented Police Patrol)*. Rockville, Md.: U.S. Department of Justice, Office of Justice Programs, National Institute of Justice. 1984.

Oettmeier, Timothy N., and William H. Bieck. *Integrating Investigative Operations Through Neighborhood-Oriented Policing: Executive Session #2.* Houston: Houston Police Department. 1987.

Oettmeier, Timothy N., and William H. Bieck. *Developing a Policing Style for Neighborhood Policing: Executive Session #1.* Houston: Houston Police Department. 1987.

Pate, Antony, and Sampson Annan. *Baltimore Community Policing Experiment Part 1— Technical Report; and Part 2—Appendixes.* Rockville, Md.: U.S. Department of Justice, Office of Justice Programs, National Institute of Justice. 1989.

Pate, Antony, and Sampson Annan. *Baltimore Community Policing Experiment: Summary Report.* Rockville, Md.: U.S. Department of Justice, Office of Justice Programs, National Institute of Justice. 1989.

Pate, Antony, Mary Ann Wycoff, Wesley Skogan, and Lawrence W. Sherman. *Reducing Fear of Crime in Houston and Newark.* New York: AMS Press Inc. 1987.

Pate, Antony, Mary Ann Wycoff, Wesley Skogan, and Lawrence W. Sherman. *Reducing Fear of Crime in Houston and Newark: A Summary Report.* Washington, D.C.: Police Foundation. 1986.

Pate, Antony and Wesley Skogan. *Coordinated Community Policing—The Newark Experience Technical Report.* Rockville, Md.: U.S. Department of Justice, Office of Justice Programs, National Institute of Justice. 1985.

Pate, Antony, P.J. Lavrakas, Mary Ann Wycoff, Wesley Skogan, and Lawrence Sherman. *Neighborhood Police Newsletters—Experiments in Newark and Houston Technical Report.* Rockville, Md.: U.S. Department of Justice, Office of Justice Programs, National Institute of Justice. 1985.

Pate, Antony, Robert Bowers, and Ron Parks. Three Approaches to Criminal Apprehension in Kansas City: An Evaluation Report. Washington, D.C.: Police Foundation. 1976.

Payne, Dennis M., and Robert C. Trojanowicz. Performance Profiles of Foot Versus Motor Officers. East Lansing, Mich.: National Neighborhood Foot Patrol Center, Michigan State University, School of Criminal Justice. 1985.

Peak, Ken, Robert Bradshaw, and Ronald Glensor. "Improving Citizen Perceptions of the Police: 'Back to the Basics' With a Community Policing Strategy." Journal of Criminal Justice 20(1) (1992).

Philadelphia Police Study Task Force. Philadelphia and Its Police: Toward a New Partnership. Philadelphia: Philadelphia Police Study Task Force. 1987.

Police Foundation. Foot Patrol—Crime Files Series. Rockville, Md.: U.S. Department of Justice, Office of Justice Programs, National Institute of Justice. 1984.

President's Commission on Law Enforcement and Administration of Justice. Task Force Report: The Police. Washington, D.C.: U.S. Government Printing Office. 1967.

President's Commission on Law Enforcement and Administration of Justice. The Challenge of Crime in a Free Society. Washington, D.C.: U.S. Government Printing Office. 1967.

Punch, Maurice, ed. Control in the Public Organization. Cambridge, Mass.: MIT Press. 1983.

Reiner, R. "Watershed in Policing." Political Quarterly (April–June 1985).

Reiss, Albert J., Jr. Private Employment of Public Force. Washington, D.C.: U.S. Department of Justice, Office of Justice Programs, National Institute of Justice. 1988.

Reiss, Albert J., Jr. Police a City's Central District: The Oakland Story. Washington, D.C.: U.S. Government Printing Office. 1985.

Reiss, Albert J., Jr. The Police and the Public. New Haven, Conn.: Yale University Press. 1971.

Richardson, J. Exploratory Study of Present and Potential Relations Between Community Policing and Neighborhood Justice Centers. Washington, D.C.: U.S. Department of Justice, Office of Justice Programs, National Institute of Justice. 1991.

Riechers, L.M., and R.R. Roiberg. "Community Policing: A Critical Review of Underlying Assumptions." Journal of Police Science and Administration 17(2) (June 1990).

Ripley, J.P. "Crime Prevention Through Community Relations." Innovations in South Carolina Law Enforcement. Rockville, Md.: U.S. Department of Justice, Office of Justice Programs, National Institute of Justice. 1982.

Ruane, J.M., and K.A. Cerulo. "Police and Community Mental Health Centers (CMHCs): The Transition From Penal to Therapeutic Control." *Law and Police* 12(2) (April 1990).

Rush, Thomas Vale. *A Study of Police-Citizen Transactions.* Dissertation. Philadelphia: Temple University. 1974.

Scanlon, Robert A., ed. *Law Enforcement Bible.* South Hackensack, N.J.: Stoeger Publishing Company. 1982.

Schnelle, John F., Robert E. Kirchner, Jr., Joe D. Casey, Paul H. Uselton, Jr., and M. Patrick McNees. "Patrol Evaluation Research: A Multiple Baseline Analysis of Saturation Police Patrolling During Day and Night Hours." *Journal of Applied Behavior Analysis* 10(1977).

Schwab, S. *Restructuring Small Police Agencies: A Transition Toward Customer Service.* Sacramento: California Commission on Peace Officer Standards and Training (POST). 1992.

Scott, Eric J. "The Impact of Victimization on Fear." *Crime and Delinquency* 31(1981).

Sechrest, et al. *Rehabilitation of Criminal Offenders* 2(1979).

Sherman, Lawrence W. *Neighborhood Safety—Crime File Series Study Guide.* Rockville, Md.: U.S. Department of Justice, Office of Justice Programs, National Institute of Justice. 1986.

Sherman, Lawrence W., Patrick R. Gartin, and Michael E. Buerger. "Hot Spots of Predatory Crime: Routing Activities and the Criminology of Place." *Criminology* 27(1) (1989).

Skogan, Wesley G. and George E. Attunes. "Information, Apprehension, and Deterrence: Exploring the Limits of Police Productivity." *Journal of Criminal Justice* 7(1979).

Skolnick, Jerome H., and David H. Bayley. *New Blue Line: Police Innovation in Six American Cities.* New York: Free Press. 1986.

Smith, Douglas A. "Neighborhood Context of Police Behavior." In *Communities and Crime,* eds. Albert J. Reiss, Jr., and Michael Tonry. Chicago: University of Chicago Press. 1986. (See NCJ 103315.)

Sparrow, Malcolm K. *Information Systems and the Development of Policing.* Perspectives on Policing. Washington, D.C.: U.S. Department of Justice, Office of Justice Programs, National Institute of Justice; and John F. Kennedy School of Government, Harvard University. 1993.

Sparrow, Malcolm K. *Implementing Community Policing.* Perspectives on Policing. Washington, D.C.: U.S. Department of Justice, Office of Justice Programs, National Institute of Justice; and John F. Kennedy School of Government, Harvard University. 1988.

Sparrow, Malcolm K., Mark H. Moore, and David M. Kennedy. *Beyond 911: A New Era for Policing.* New York: Basic Books, Inc. 1990.

Staff report to the National Commission on the Causes and Prevention of Violence. Law and Order Reconsidered. Washington, D.C.: U.S. Government Printing Office. 1969.

Stratta, E. "Lack of Consultation." Policing 6(3) (Autumn 1990).

Taylor, M. "Constraints to Community-Oriented Policing." Police Journal 15(2) (April 1992).

Toch, Hans, and J. Douglas Grant. Police As Problem Solvers. New York: Plenum Publishing Corporations. 1991.

Trojanowicz, Robert C. Preventing Civil Disturbances: A Community Policing Approach. Washington, D.C.: U.S. Department of Justice, Office of Justice Programs, National Institute of Justice. 1989.

Trojanowicz, Robert C. An Evaluation of a Neighborhood Foot Patrol Program in Flint, Michigan. East Lansing, Mich.: Michigan State University. 1982.

Trojanowicz, Robert C. "An Evaluation of a Neighborhood Foot Patrol Program." Journal of Police Science Administration 11(4) (December 1983).

Trojanowicz, Robert C., and Bonnie Bucqueroux. Toward Development of Meaningful and Effective Performance Evaluations. East Lansing, Mich.: National Center for Community Policing, Michigan State University School of Criminal Justice. 1992.

Trojanowicz, Robert C., and Bonnie Bucqueroux. Community Policing and the Challenge of Diversity. Washington, D.C.: U.S. Department of Justice, Office of Justice Programs, National Institute of Justice. 1991.

Trojanowicz, Robert C., and Bonnie Bucqueroux. Community Policing. Cincinnati, Ohio: Anderson Publishing Company. 1990.

Trojanowicz, Robert C., and Mark H. Moore The Meaning of Community in Community Policing. East Lansing, Mich.: Michigan State University, National Neighborhood Foot Patrol Center, School of Criminal Justice. 1988.

Trojanowicz, Robert C., and David Carter. Philosophy and Role of Community Policing. Rockville, Md.: U.S. Department of Justice, Office of Justice Programs, National Institute of Justice. 1988.

Trojanowicz, Robert C., B. Benson, and Susan Trojanowicz. Community Policing: University Input Into Campus Police Policy-Making. East Lansing, Mich.: National Neighborhood Foot Patrol Center, Michigan State University, School of Criminal Justice. 1988.

Trojanowicz, Robert C., Richard Gleason, Bonnie Pollard, and David Sinclair. Community Policing: Community Input Into Police Policy-Making. East Lansing, Mich.: National Neighborhood Foot Patrol Center, Michigan State University, School of Criminal Justice. 1987.

Trojanowicz, Robert C., and Bonnie Pollard. *Community Policing: The Line Officer's Perspective.* East Lansing, Mich.: National Neighborhood Foot Patrol Center, Michigan State University, School of Criminal Justice. 1986.

Trojanowicz, Robert C., Marilyn Steele, and Susan Trojanowicz. *Community Policing: A Taxpayer's Perspective.* East Lansing, Mich.: National Neighborhood Foot Patrol Center, Michigan State University, School of Criminal Justice. 1986.

Trojanowicz, Robert C., Bonnie Pollard, Francine Colgan, and Hazel A. Harden. *Community Policing Programs—A Twenty-Year View.* East Lansing, Mich.: National Neighborhood Foot Patrol Center, Michigan State University, School of Criminal Justice. 1986.

Trojanowicz, Robert C., and Jerome Belknap. *Community Policing: Training Issues.* East Lansing, Mich.: National Neighborhood Foot Patrol Center, Michigan State University, School of Criminal Justice. 1986.

Trojanowicz, Robert C., and Dennis W. Banas. *Perceptions of Safety: A Comparison of Foot Patrol Versus Motor Patrol Officers.* East Lansing, Mich.: National Neighborhood Foot Patrol Center, Michigan State University, School of Criminal Justice. 1985.

Trojanowicz, Robert C., and Dennis W. Banas. *Job Satisfaction: A Comparison of Foot Patrol Versus Motor Patrol Officers.* East Lansing, Mich.: National Neighborhood Foot Patrol Center, Michigan State University, School of Criminal Justice. 1985.

Trojanowicz, Robert C., and Dennis W. Banas. *Impact of Foot Patrol on Black and White Perceptions of Policing.* East Lansing, Mich.: National Neighborhood Foot Patrol Center, Michigan State University, School of Criminal Justice. 1985.

Trojanowicz, Robert C., and Hazel A. Harden. *Status of Contemporary Community Policing Programs.* East Lansing, Mich.: National Neighborhood Foot Patrol Center, Michigan State University, School of Criminal Justice. 1985.

Trojanowicz, Robert C., and P.R. Smyth. *Manual for the Establishment and Operation of a Foot Patrol Program.* East Lansing, Mich.: National Neighborhood Foot Patrol Center, Michigan State University, School of Criminal Justice. 1984.

Tucson Police Department. *Tucson Police Department Enhanced Crime Prevention Program, Final Report.* Tucson, Ariz.: Tucson Police Department. 1991.

Turner, B. "Community Policing: Beyond Neighborhood Watch." *Research Update* 2(4) (Fall 1991).

Uchida, Craig, Brian Forst, and Sampson Annan. *Modern Policing and the Control of Illegal Drugs: Testing New Strategies in Two American Cities.* Washington, D.C.: Police Foundation. 1992.

United States Conference of Mayors. *Directory of City Policing Programs, Volume IV.* Rockville, Md.: U.S. Department of Justice, Office of Justice Programs, National Institute of Justice. 1990.

University of South Carolina College of Criminal Justice. *Innovations in South Carolina Law Enforcement, 1985.* Rockville, Md.: U.S. Department of Justice, Office of Justice Programs, National Institute of Justice. 1985.

Vaughn, J.R. "Community-Oriented Policing . . . You Can Make It Happen." *Law and Order* 39(6) (June 1991).

Wadman, Robert C., and Robert K. Olson. *Community Wellness: A New Theory of Policing.* Washington, D.C.: Police Executive Research Forum. 1990.

Ward, J. "Community Policing on the Home Front." *CJ the Americas* 5(2) (April–May 1992).

Wasserman, Robert, and Mark H. Moore. *Values in Policing.* Perspectives on Policing. Washington, D.C.: U.S. Department of Justice, Office of Justice Programs, National Institute of Justice; and John F. Kennedy School of Government, Harvard University. 1988.

Webber, Alan M. "Crime and Management: An Interview With New York City Police Commissioner Lee P. Brown." *Harvard Business Review* 69(May–June 1991).

Weisburd, David, Jerome McElroy, and Patricia Hardyman. "Challenges to Supervision in Community Policing: Observations on a Pilot Project." *American Journal of Police* 7(2) (1988).

Whitaker, Gordon P., ed. *Understanding Police Agency Performance.* Washington, D.C.: Government Printing Office. 1984.

Wiatrowski, M., and J. Vardalis. "Experiment in Community Policing in Delray Beach, Florida." *Police Journal* 63(2) (April–June 1990).

Williams, Hubert, and Patrick V. Murphy. *The Evolving Strategy of Police: A Minority View.* Perspectives on Policing. Washington, D.C.: U.S. Department of Justice, Office of Justice Programs, National Institute of Justice; and John F. Kennedy School of Government, Harvard University. 1990.

Wilson, James Q., and George L. Kelling. "Making Neighborhoods Safe." *The Atlantic Monthly* 263(2) (February 1989).

Wilson, James Q. and George L. Kelling. "Broken Windows." *The Atlantic Monthly* (March 1982).

Witte, Jeffrey E., Lawrence F. Travis III, and Robert H. Langworthy. "Participatory Management in Law Enforcement: Police Officer, Supervisor, and Administrator Perceptions." *American Journal of Police* 9(4) (1990).

Wycoff, Mary Ann, and Timothy N. Oettmeier. Planning and Implementation Issues for Community-Oriented Policing: The Houston Experience. Washington, D.C.: U.S. Department of Justice, Office of Justice Programs, National Institute of Justice. Forthcoming.

Wycoff, Mary Ann, and Wesley G. Skogan. Community Policing: Quality From the Inside, Out. Washington, D.C.: U.S. Department of Justice, Office of Justice Programs, National Institute of Justice. Forthcoming.

Wycoff, Mary Ann, and Wesley G. Skogan. Citizen Contact Patrol—The Houston Field Test. Washington, D.C.: Police Foundation; and Rockville, Md.: U.S. Department of Justice, Office of Justice Programs, National Institute of Justice. 1985.

Wycoff, Mary Ann, Wesley G. Skogan, Anthony M. Pate, and Lawrence W. Sherman. Police Community Stations: The Houston Field Test, Executive Summary. Rockville, Md.: U.S. Department of Justice, Office of Justice Programs, National Institute of Justice. 1985.

Wycoff, Mary Ann, Wesley G. Skogan, Anthony M. Pate, and Lawrence W. Sherman. Police as Community Organizers—The Houston Field Test, Executive Summary. Rockville, Md.: U.S. Department of Justice, Office of Justice Programs, National Institute of Justice. 1985.

Wycoff, Mary Ann, and Wesley G. Skogan. Police as Community Organizers—The Houston Field Test, Technical Report. Washington, D.C.: Police Foundation; and Rockville, Md.: U.S. Department of Justice, Office of Justice Programs, National Institute of Justice. 1985.